Running Log Book

by

_____

_____

_____

Year: .... Month: .... Week: .... Weekly Goal: ....

Monday	Date:	Burns Target:
Notes:	Route:	
	Distance:	Time:
	Weight:	Speed:
	Burn Cals:	Heart Rate:
	Weather:	Breathing:
	How I Felt:	
	Injuries:	
	Overall Thoughts:	

Tuesday	Date:	Burns Target:
Notes:	Route:	
	Distance:	Time:
	Weight:	Speed:
	Burn Cals:	Heart Rate:
	Weather:	Breathing:
	How I Felt:	
	Injuries:	
	Overall Thoughts:	

Wednesday	Date:	Burns Target:
Notes:	Route:	
	Distance:	Time:
	Weight:	Speed:
	Burn Cals:	Heart Rate:
	Weather:	Breathing:
	How I Felt:	
	Injuries:	
	Overall Thoughts:	

Thursday	Date:	Burns Target:
Notes:	Route:	
	Distance:	Time:
	Weight:	Speed:
	Burn Cals:	Heart Rate:
	Weather:	Breathing:
	How I Felt:	
	Injuries:	
	Overall Thoughts:	

Friday	Date:	Burns Target:
Notes:	Route:	
	Distance:	Time:
	Weight:	Speed:
	Burn Cals:	Heart Rate:
	Weather:	Breathing:
	How I Felt:	
	Injuries:	
	Overall Thoughts:	

Saturday	Date:	Burns Target:
Notes:	Route:	
	Distance:	Time:
	Weight:	Speed:
	Burn Cals:	Heart Rate:
	Weather:	Breathing:
	How I Felt:	
	Injuries:	
	Overall Thoughts:	

Sunday	Date:	Burns Target:
Notes:	Route:	
	Distance:	Time:
	Weight:	Speed:
	Burn Cals:	Heart Rate:
	Weather:	Breathing:
	How I Felt:	
	Injuries:	
	Overall Thoughts:	

Weekly Review

Total Distance:		Weight loss:	
Average Speed:		Total Hours:	
Average Heart Rate:		Total Burns:	

Notes / Thoughts:

Year:_____ Month:_____ Week:_____ Weekly Goal:_____

Monday	Date:		Burns Target:
Notes:	Route:		
	Distance:	Time:	
	Weight:	Speed:	
	Burn Cals:	Heart Rate:	
	Weather:	Breathing:	
	How I Felt:		
	Injuries:		
	Overall Thoughts:		

Tuesday	Date:		Burns Target:
Notes:	Route:		
	Distance:	Time:	
	Weight:	Speed:	
	Burn Cals:	Heart Rate:	
	Weather:	Breathing:	
	How I Felt:		
	Injuries:		
	Overall Thoughts:		

Wednesday	Date:		Burns Target:
Notes:	Route:		
	Distance:	Time:	
	Weight:	Speed:	
	Burn Cals:	Heart Rate:	
	Weather:	Breathing:	
	How I Felt:		
	Injuries:		
	Overall Thoughts:		

Thursday	Date:		Burns Target:
Notes:	Route:		
	Distance:	Time:	
	Weight:	Speed:	
	Burn Cals:	Heart Rate:	
	Weather:	Breathing:	
	How I Felt:		
	Injuries:		
	Overall Thoughts:		

Friday	Date:		Burns Target:	
Notes:	Route:			
	Distance:		Time:	
	Weight:		Speed:	
	Burn Cals:		Heart Rate:	
	Weather:		Breathing:	
	How I Felt:			
	Injuries:			
	Overall Thoughts:			

Saturday	Date:		Burns Target:	
Notes:	Route:			
	Distance:		Time:	
	Weight:		Speed:	
	Burn Cals:		Heart Rate:	
	Weather:		Breathing:	
	How I Felt:			
	Injuries:			
	Overall Thoughts:			

Sunday	Date:		Burns Target:	
Notes:	Route:			
	Distance:		Time:	
	Weight:		Speed:	
	Burn Cals:		Heart Rate:	
	Weather:		Breathing:	
	How I Felt:			
	Injuries:			
	Overall Thoughts:			

Weekly Review

Total Distance:		Weight loss:	
Average Speed:		Total Hours:	
Average Heart Rate:		Total Burns:	

Notes / Thoughts:

Year:_____ Month:_____ Week:_____ Weekly Goal:_____

Monday	**Date:**	**Burns Target:**
Notes:	Route:	
	Distance:	Time:
	Weight:	Speed:
	Burn Cals:	Heart Rate:
	Weather:	Breathing:
	How I Felt:	
	Injuries:	
	Overall Thoughts:	

Tuesday	**Date:**	**Burns Target:**
Notes:	Route:	
	Distance:	Time:
	Weight:	Speed:
	Burn Cals:	Heart Rate:
	Weather:	Breathing:
	How I Felt:	
	Injuries:	
	Overall Thoughts:	

Wednesday	**Date:**	**Burns Target:**
Notes:	Route:	
	Distance:	Time:
	Weight:	Speed:
	Burn Cals:	Heart Rate:
	Weather:	Breathing:
	How I Felt:	
	Injuries:	
	Overall Thoughts:	

Thursday	**Date:**	**Burns Target:**
Notes:	Route:	
	Distance:	Time:
	Weight:	Speed:
	Burn Cals:	Heart Rate:
	Weather:	Breathing:
	How I Felt:	
	Injuries:	
	Overall Thoughts:	

Friday	Date:		Burns Target:	
Notes:	Route:			
	Distance:		Time:	
	Weight:		Speed:	
	Burn Cals:		Heart Rate:	
	Weather:		Breathing:	
	How I Felt:			
	Injuries:			
	Overall Thoughts:			

Saturday	Date:		Burns Target:	
Notes:	Route:			
	Distance:		Time:	
	Weight:		Speed:	
	Burn Cals:		Heart Rate:	
	Weather:		Breathing:	
	How I Felt:			
	Injuries:			
	Overall Thoughts:			

Sunday	Date:		Burns Target:	
Notes:	Route:			
	Distance:		Time:	
	Weight:		Speed:	
	Burn Cals:		Heart Rate:	
	Weather:		Breathing:	
	How I Felt:			
	Injuries:			
	Overall Thoughts:			

Weekly Review			
Total Distance:		Weight loss:	
Average Speed:		Total Hours:	
Average Heart Rate:		Total Burns:	
Notes / Thoughts:			

Year: _____ Month: _____ Week: _____ Weekly Goal: _____

Monday	Date:	Burns Target:
Notes:	Route:	
	Distance:	Time:
	Weight:	Speed:
	Burn Cals:	Heart Rate:
	Weather:	Breathing:
	How I Felt:	
	Injuries:	
	Overall Thoughts:	

Tuesday	Date:	Burns Target:
Notes:	Route:	
	Distance:	Time:
	Weight:	Speed:
	Burn Cals:	Heart Rate:
	Weather:	Breathing:
	How I Felt:	
	Injuries:	
	Overall Thoughts:	

Wednesday	Date:	Burns Target:
Notes:	Route:	
	Distance:	Time:
	Weight:	Speed:
	Burn Cals:	Heart Rate:
	Weather:	Breathing:
	How I Felt:	
	Injuries:	
	Overall Thoughts:	

Thursday	Date:	Burns Target:
Notes:	Route:	
	Distance:	Time:
	Weight:	Speed:
	Burn Cals:	Heart Rate:
	Weather:	Breathing:
	How I Felt:	
	Injuries:	
	Overall Thoughts:	

Friday	Date:		Burns Target:	
Notes:	Route:			
	Distance:		Time:	
	Weight:		Speed:	
	Burn Cals:		Heart Rate:	
	Weather:		Breathing:	
	How I Felt:			
	Injuries:			
	Overall Thoughts:			

Saturday	Date:		Burns Target:	
Notes:	Route:			
	Distance:		Time:	
	Weight:		Speed:	
	Burn Cals:		Heart Rate:	
	Weather:		Breathing:	
	How I Felt:			
	Injuries:			
	Overall Thoughts:			

Sunday	Date:		Burns Target:	
Notes:	Route:			
	Distance:		Time:	
	Weight:		Speed:	
	Burn Cals:		Heart Rate:	
	Weather:		Breathing:	
	How I Felt:			
	Injuries:			
	Overall Thoughts:			

Weekly Review

Total Distance:		Weight loss:	
Average Speed:		Total Hours:	
Average Heart Rate:		Total Burns:	

Notes / Thoughts:

Year:_____ Month:_____ Week:_____ Weekly Goal:_____

Monday	Date:	Burns Target:	
Notes:	Route:		
	Distance:	Time:	
	Weight:	Speed:	
	Burn Cals:	Heart Rate:	
	Weather:	Breathing:	
	How I Felt:		
	Injuries:		
	Overall Thoughts:		

Tuesday	Date:	Burns Target:	
Notes:	Route:		
	Distance:	Time:	
	Weight:	Speed:	
	Burn Cals:	Heart Rate:	
	Weather:	Breathing:	
	How I Felt:		
	Injuries:		
	Overall Thoughts:		

Wednesday	Date:	Burns Target:	
Notes:	Route:		
	Distance:	Time:	
	Weight:	Speed:	
	Burn Cals:	Heart Rate:	
	Weather:	Breathing:	
	How I Felt:		
	Injuries:		
	Overall Thoughts:		

Thursday	Date:	Burns Target:	
Notes:	Route:		
	Distance:	Time:	
	Weight:	Speed:	
	Burn Cals:	Heart Rate:	
	Weather:	Breathing:	
	How I Felt:		
	Injuries:		
	Overall Thoughts:		

Friday	Date:	Burns Target:	
Notes:	Route:		
	Distance:	Time:	
	Weight:	Speed:	
	Burn Cals:	Heart Rate:	
	Weather:	Breathing:	
	How I Felt:		
	Injuries:		
	Overall Thoughts:		

Saturday	Date:	Burns Target:	
Notes:	Route:		
	Distance:	Time:	
	Weight:	Speed:	
	Burn Cals:	Heart Rate:	
	Weather:	Breathing:	
	How I Felt:		
	Injuries:		
	Overall Thoughts:		

Sunday	Date:	Burns Target:	
Notes:	Route:		
	Distance:	Time:	
	Weight:	Speed:	
	Burn Cals:	Heart Rate:	
	Weather:	Breathing:	
	How I Felt:		
	Injuries:		
	Overall Thoughts:		

Weekly Review

Total Distance:		Weight loss:	
Average Speed:		Total Hours:	
Average Heart Rate:		Total Burns:	

Notes / Thoughts:

Year:_____ Month:_____ Week:_____ Weekly Goal:_____

Monday	Date:	Burns Target:	
Notes:	Route:		
	Distance:	Time:	
	Weight:	Speed:	
	Burn Cals:	Heart Rate:	
	Weather:	Breathing:	
	How I Felt:		
	Injuries:		
	Overall Thoughts:		

Tuesday	Date:	Burns Target:	
Notes:	Route:		
	Distance:	Time:	
	Weight:	Speed:	
	Burn Cals:	Heart Rate:	
	Weather:	Breathing:	
	How I Felt:		
	Injuries:		
	Overall Thoughts:		

Wednesday	Date:	Burns Target:	
Notes:	Route:		
	Distance:	Time:	
	Weight:	Speed:	
	Burn Cals:	Heart Rate:	
	Weather:	Breathing:	
	How I Felt:		
	Injuries:		
	Overall Thoughts:		

Thursday	Date:	Burns Target:	
Notes:	Route:		
	Distance:	Time:	
	Weight:	Speed:	
	Burn Cals:	Heart Rate:	
	Weather:	Breathing:	
	How I Felt:		
	Injuries:		
	Overall Thoughts:		

Friday	Date:		Burns Target:
Notes:	Route:		
	Distance:	Time:	
	Weight:	Speed:	
	Burn Cals:	Heart Rate:	
	Weather:	Breathing:	
	How I Felt:		
	Injuries:		
	Overall Thoughts:		

Saturday	Date:		Burns Target:
Notes:	Route:		
	Distance:	Time:	
	Weight:	Speed:	
	Burn Cals:	Heart Rate:	
	Weather:	Breathing:	
	How I Felt:		
	Injuries:		
	Overall Thoughts:		

Sunday	Date:		Burns Target:
Notes:	Route:		
	Distance:	Time:	
	Weight:	Speed:	
	Burn Cals:	Heart Rate:	
	Weather:	Breathing:	
	How I Felt:		
	Injuries:		
	Overall Thoughts:		

Weekly Review

Total Distance:		Weight loss:	
Average Speed:		Total Hours:	
Average Heart Rate:		Total Burns:	

Notes / Thoughts:

Year: _____ Month: _____ Week: _____ Weekly Goal: _____

Monday	Date:	Burns Target:	
Notes:	Route:		
	Distance:	Time:	
	Weight:	Speed:	
	Burn Cals:	Heart Rate:	
	Weather:	Breathing:	
	How I Felt:		
	Injuries:		
	Overall Thoughts:		

Tuesday	Date:	Burns Target:	
Notes:	Route:		
	Distance:	Time:	
	Weight:	Speed:	
	Burn Cals:	Heart Rate:	
	Weather:	Breathing:	
	How I Felt:		
	Injuries:		
	Overall Thoughts:		

Wednesday	Date:	Burns Target:	
Notes:	Route:		
	Distance:	Time:	
	Weight:	Speed:	
	Burn Cals:	Heart Rate:	
	Weather:	Breathing:	
	How I Felt:		
	Injuries:		
	Overall Thoughts:		

Thursday	Date:	Burns Target:	
Notes:	Route:		
	Distance:	Time:	
	Weight:	Speed:	
	Burn Cals:	Heart Rate:	
	Weather:	Breathing:	
	How I Felt:		
	Injuries:		
	Overall Thoughts:		

Friday	Date:		Burns Target:	
Notes:	Route:			
	Distance:		Time:	
	Weight:		Speed:	
	Burn Cals:		Heart Rate:	
	Weather:		Breathing:	
	How I Felt:			
	Injuries:			
	Overall Thoughts:			

Saturday	Date:		Burns Target:	
Notes:	Route:			
	Distance:		Time:	
	Weight:		Speed:	
	Burn Cals:		Heart Rate:	
	Weather:		Breathing:	
	How I Felt:			
	Injuries:			
	Overall Thoughts:			

Sunday	Date:		Burns Target:	
Notes:	Route:			
	Distance:		Time:	
	Weight:		Speed:	
	Burn Cals:		Heart Rate:	
	Weather:		Breathing:	
	How I Felt:			
	Injuries:			
	Overall Thoughts:			

Weekly Review

Total Distance:		Weight loss:	
Average Speed:		Total Hours:	
Average Heart Rate:		Total Burns:	

Notes / Thoughts:

Year:_____ Month:_____ Week:_____ Weekly Goal:_____

Monday	**Date:**		**Burns Target:**
Notes:	Route:		
	Distance:	Time:	
	Weight:	Speed:	
	Burn Cals:	Heart Rate:	
	Weather:	Breathing:	
	How I Felt:		
	Injuries:		
	Overall Thoughts:		

Tuesday	**Date:**		**Burns Target:**
Notes:	Route:		
	Distance:	Time:	
	Weight:	Speed:	
	Burn Cals:	Heart Rate:	
	Weather:	Breathing:	
	How I Felt:		
	Injuries:		
	Overall Thoughts:		

Wednesday	**Date:**		**Burns Target:**
Notes:	Route:		
	Distance:	Time:	
	Weight:	Speed:	
	Burn Cals:	Heart Rate:	
	Weather:	Breathing:	
	How I Felt:		
	Injuries:		
	Overall Thoughts:		

Thursday	**Date:**		**Burns Target:**
Notes:	Route:		
	Distance:	Time:	
	Weight:	Speed:	
	Burn Cals:	Heart Rate:	
	Weather:	Breathing:	
	How I Felt:		
	Injuries:		
	Overall Thoughts:		

Friday	Date:		Burns Target:	
Notes:	Route:			
	Distance:		Time:	
	Weight:		Speed:	
	Burn Cals:		Heart Rate:	
	Weather:		Breathing:	
	How I Felt:			
	Injuries:			
	Overall Thoughts:			

Saturday	Date:		Burns Target:	
Notes:	Route:			
	Distance:		Time:	
	Weight:		Speed:	
	Burn Cals:		Heart Rate:	
	Weather:		Breathing:	
	How I Felt:			
	Injuries:			
	Overall Thoughts:			

Sunday	Date:		Burns Target:	
Notes:	Route:			
	Distance:		Time:	
	Weight:		Speed:	
	Burn Cals:		Heart Rate:	
	Weather:		Breathing:	
	How I Felt:			
	Injuries:			
	Overall Thoughts:			

Weekly Review

Total Distance:		Weight loss:	
Average Speed:		Total Hours:	
Average Heart Rate:		Total Burns:	

Notes / Thoughts:

Year:............ Month:............ Week:............ Weekly Goal:.........

Monday	Date:	Burns Target:
Notes:	Route:	
	Distance:	Time:
	Weight:	Speed:
	Burn Cals:	Heart Rate:
	Weather:	Breathing:
	How I Felt:	
	Injuries:	
	Overall Thoughts:	

Tuesday	Date:	Burns Target:
Notes:	Route:	
	Distance:	Time:
	Weight:	Speed:
	Burn Cals:	Heart Rate:
	Weather:	Breathing:
	How I Felt:	
	Injuries:	
	Overall Thoughts:	

Wednesday	Date:	Burns Target:
Notes:	Route:	
	Distance:	Time:
	Weight:	Speed:
	Burn Cals:	Heart Rate:
	Weather:	Breathing:
	How I Felt:	
	Injuries:	
	Overall Thoughts:	

Thursday	Date:	Burns Target:
Notes:	Route:	
	Distance:	Time:
	Weight:	Speed:
	Burn Cals:	Heart Rate:
	Weather:	Breathing:
	How I Felt:	
	Injuries:	
	Overall Thoughts:	

Friday	Date:		Burns Target:	
Notes:	Route:			
	Distance:		Time:	
	Weight:		Speed:	
	Burn Cals:		Heart Rate:	
	Weather:		Breathing:	
	How I Felt:			
	Injuries:			
	Overall Thoughts:			

Saturday	Date:		Burns Target:	
Notes:	Route:			
	Distance:		Time:	
	Weight:		Speed:	
	Burn Cals:		Heart Rate:	
	Weather:		Breathing:	
	How I Felt:			
	Injuries:			
	Overall Thoughts:			

Sunday	Date:		Burns Target:	
Notes:	Route:			
	Distance:		Time:	
	Weight:		Speed:	
	Burn Cals:		Heart Rate:	
	Weather:		Breathing:	
	How I Felt:			
	Injuries:			
	Overall Thoughts:			

Weekly Review

Total Distance:		Weight loss:	
Average Speed:		Total Hours:	
Average Heart Rate:		Total Burns:	

Notes / Thoughts:

Year: _____ Month: _____ Week: _____ Weekly Goal: _____

Monday	Date:		Burns Target:	
Notes:	Route:			
	Distance:		Time:	
	Weight:		Speed:	
	Burn Cals:		Heart Rate:	
	Weather:		Breathing:	
	How I Felt:			
	Injuries:			
	Overall Thoughts:			

Tuesday	Date:		Burns Target:	
Notes:	Route:			
	Distance:		Time:	
	Weight:		Speed:	
	Burn Cals:		Heart Rate:	
	Weather:		Breathing:	
	How I Felt:			
	Injuries:			
	Overall Thoughts:			

Wednesday	Date:		Burns Target:	
Notes:	Route:			
	Distance:		Time:	
	Weight:		Speed:	
	Burn Cals:		Heart Rate:	
	Weather:		Breathing:	
	How I Felt:			
	Injuries:			
	Overall Thoughts:			

Thursday	Date:		Burns Target:	
Notes:	Route:			
	Distance:		Time:	
	Weight:		Speed:	
	Burn Cals:		Heart Rate:	
	Weather:		Breathing:	
	How I Felt:			
	Injuries:			
	Overall Thoughts:			

Friday	Date:		Burns Target:	
Notes:	Route:			
	Distance:		Time:	
	Weight:		Speed:	
	Burn Cals:		Heart Rate:	
	Weather:		Breathing:	
	How I Felt:			
	Injuries:			
	Overall Thoughts:			

Saturday	Date:		Burns Target:	
Notes:	Route:			
	Distance:		Time:	
	Weight:		Speed:	
	Burn Cals:		Heart Rate:	
	Weather:		Breathing:	
	How I Felt:			
	Injuries:			
	Overall Thoughts:			

Sunday	Date:		Burns Target:	
Notes:	Route:			
	Distance:		Time:	
	Weight:		Speed:	
	Burn Cals:		Heart Rate:	
	Weather:		Breathing:	
	How I Felt:			
	Injuries:			
	Overall Thoughts:			

Weekly Review

Total Distance:		Weight loss:	
Average Speed:		Total Hours:	
Average Heart Rate:		Total Burns:	

Notes / Thoughts:

Year:_____ Month:_____ Week:_____ Weekly Goal:_____

Monday	Date:	Burns Target:
Notes:	Route:	
	Distance:	Time:
	Weight:	Speed:
	Burn Cals:	Heart Rate:
	Weather:	Breathing:
	How I Felt:	
	Injuries:	
	Overall Thoughts:	

Tuesday	Date:	Burns Target:
Notes:	Route:	
	Distance:	Time:
	Weight:	Speed:
	Burn Cals:	Heart Rate:
	Weather:	Breathing:
	How I Felt:	
	Injuries:	
	Overall Thoughts:	

Wednesday	Date:	Burns Target:
Notes:	Route:	
	Distance:	Time:
	Weight:	Speed:
	Burn Cals:	Heart Rate:
	Weather:	Breathing:
	How I Felt:	
	Injuries:	
	Overall Thoughts:	

Thursday	Date:	Burns Target:
Notes:	Route:	
	Distance:	Time:
	Weight:	Speed:
	Burn Cals:	Heart Rate:
	Weather:	Breathing:
	How I Felt:	
	Injuries:	
	Overall Thoughts:	

Friday	Date:		Burns Target:	
Notes:	Route:			
	Distance:		Time:	
	Weight:		Speed:	
	Burn Cals:		Heart Rate:	
	Weather:		Breathing:	
	How I Felt:			
	Injuries:			
	Overall Thoughts:			

Saturday	Date:		Burns Target:	
Notes:	Route:			
	Distance:		Time:	
	Weight:		Speed:	
	Burn Cals:		Heart Rate:	
	Weather:		Breathing:	
	How I Felt:			
	Injuries:			
	Overall Thoughts:			

Sunday	Date:		Burns Target:	
Notes:	Route:			
	Distance:		Time:	
	Weight:		Speed:	
	Burn Cals:		Heart Rate:	
	Weather:		Breathing:	
	How I Felt:			
	Injuries:			
	Overall Thoughts:			

Weekly Review

Total Distance:		Weight loss:	
Average Speed:		Total Hours:	
Average Heart Rate:		Total Burns:	

Notes / Thoughts:

Year:_____ Month:_____ Week:_____ Weekly Goal:_____

Monday	**Date:**		**Burns Target:**	
Notes:	Route:			
	Distance:		Time:	
	Weight:		Speed:	
	Burn Cals:		Heart Rate:	
	Weather:		Breathing:	
	How I Felt:			
	Injuries:			
	Overall Thoughts:			

Tuesday	**Date:**		**Burns Target:**	
Notes:	Route:			
	Distance:		Time:	
	Weight:		Speed:	
	Burn Cals:		Heart Rate:	
	Weather:		Breathing:	
	How I Felt:			
	Injuries:			
	Overall Thoughts:			

Wednesday	**Date:**		**Burns Target:**	
Notes:	Route:			
	Distance:		Time:	
	Weight:		Speed:	
	Burn Cals:		Heart Rate:	
	Weather:		Breathing:	
	How I Felt:			
	Injuries:			
	Overall Thoughts:			

Thursday	**Date:**		**Burns Target:**	
Notes:	Route:			
	Distance:		Time:	
	Weight:		Speed:	
	Burn Cals:		Heart Rate:	
	Weather:		Breathing:	
	How I Felt:			
	Injuries:			
	Overall Thoughts:			

Friday	Date:		Burns Target:	
Notes:	Route:			
	Distance:		Time:	
	Weight:		Speed:	
	Burn Cals:		Heart Rate:	
	Weather:		Breathing:	
	How I Felt:			
	Injuries:			
	Overall Thoughts:			

Saturday	Date:		Burns Target:	
Notes:	Route:			
	Distance:		Time:	
	Weight:		Speed:	
	Burn Cals:		Heart Rate:	
	Weather:		Breathing:	
	How I Felt:			
	Injuries:			
	Overall Thoughts:			

Sunday	Date:		Burns Target:	
Notes:	Route:			
	Distance:		Time:	
	Weight:		Speed:	
	Burn Cals:		Heart Rate:	
	Weather:		Breathing:	
	How I Felt:			
	Injuries:			
	Overall Thoughts:			

Weekly Review

Total Distance:		Weight loss:	
Average Speed:		Total Hours:	
Average Heart Rate:		Total Burns:	

Notes / Thoughts:

Year: .... Month: .... Week: .... Weekly Goal: ....

Monday	Date:	Burns Target:

Notes:

Route:
Distance: | Time:
Weight: | Speed:
Burn Cals: | Heart Rate:
Weather: | Breathing:
How I Felt:
Injuries:
Overall Thoughts:

Tuesday	Date:	Burns Target:

Notes:

Route:
Distance: | Time:
Weight: | Speed:
Burn Cals: | Heart Rate:
Weather: | Breathing:
How I Felt:
Injuries:
Overall Thoughts:

Wednesday	Date:	Burns Target:

Notes:

Route:
Distance: | Time:
Weight: | Speed:
Burn Cals: | Heart Rate:
Weather: | Breathing:
How I Felt:
Injuries:
Overall Thoughts:

Thursday	Date:	Burns Target:

Notes:

Route:
Distance: | Time:
Weight: | Speed:
Burn Cals: | Heart Rate:
Weather: | Breathing:
How I Felt:
Injuries:
Overall Thoughts:

Friday	Date:	Burns Target:	
Notes:	Route:		
	Distance:	Time:	
	Weight:	Speed:	
	Burn Cals:	Heart Rate:	
	Weather:	Breathing:	
	How I Felt:		
	Injuries:		
	Overall Thoughts:		

Saturday	Date:	Burns Target:	
Notes:	Route:		
	Distance:	Time:	
	Weight:	Speed:	
	Burn Cals:	Heart Rate:	
	Weather:	Breathing:	
	How I Felt:		
	Injuries:		
	Overall Thoughts:		

Sunday	Date:	Burns Target:	
Notes:	Route:		
	Distance:	Time:	
	Weight:	Speed:	
	Burn Cals:	Heart Rate:	
	Weather:	Breathing:	
	How I Felt:		
	Injuries:		
	Overall Thoughts:		

Weekly Review

Total Distance:		Weight loss:	
Average Speed:		Total Hours:	
Average Heart Rate:		Total Burns:	

Notes / Thoughts:

Year: _____ Month: _____ Week: _____ Weekly Goal: _____

Monday	Date:		**Burns Target:**
Notes:	Route:		
	Distance:	Time:	
	Weight:	Speed:	
	Burn Cals:	Heart Rate:	
	Weather:	Breathing:	
	How I Felt:		
	Injuries:		
	Overall Thoughts:		

Tuesday	Date:		**Burns Target:**
Notes:	Route:		
	Distance:	Time:	
	Weight:	Speed:	
	Burn Cals:	Heart Rate:	
	Weather:	Breathing:	
	How I Felt:		
	Injuries:		
	Overall Thoughts:		

Wednesday	Date:		**Burns Target:**
Notes:	Route:		
	Distance:	Time:	
	Weight:	Speed:	
	Burn Cals:	Heart Rate:	
	Weather:	Breathing:	
	How I Felt:		
	Injuries:		
	Overall Thoughts:		

Thursday	Date:		**Burns Target:**
Notes:	Route:		
	Distance:	Time:	
	Weight:	Speed:	
	Burn Cals:	Heart Rate:	
	Weather:	Breathing:	
	How I Felt:		
	Injuries:		
	Overall Thoughts:		

Friday	Date:		Burns Target:	
Notes:	Route:			
	Distance:		Time:	
	Weight:		Speed:	
	Burn Cals:		Heart Rate:	
	Weather:		Breathing:	
	How I Felt:			
	Injuries:			
	Overall Thoughts:			

Saturday	Date:		Burns Target:	
Notes:	Route:			
	Distance:		Time:	
	Weight:		Speed:	
	Burn Cals:		Heart Rate:	
	Weather:		Breathing:	
	How I Felt:			
	Injuries:			
	Overall Thoughts:			

Sunday	Date:		Burns Target:	
Notes:	Route:			
	Distance:		Time:	
	Weight:		Speed:	
	Burn Cals:		Heart Rate:	
	Weather:		Breathing:	
	How I Felt:			
	Injuries:			
	Overall Thoughts:			

Weekly Review

Total Distance:		Weight loss:	
Average Speed:		Total Hours:	
Average Heart Rate:		Total Burns:	

Notes / Thoughts:

Year:_____ Month:_____ Week:_____ Weekly Goal:_____

Monday	Date:	Burns Target:
Notes:	Route:	
	Distance:	Time:
	Weight:	Speed:
	Burn Cals:	Heart Rate:
	Weather:	Breathing:
	How I Felt:	
	Injuries:	
	Overall Thoughts:	

Tuesday	Date:	Burns Target:
Notes:	Route:	
	Distance:	Time:
	Weight:	Speed:
	Burn Cals:	Heart Rate:
	Weather:	Breathing:
	How I Felt:	
	Injuries:	
	Overall Thoughts:	

Wednesday	Date:	Burns Target:
Notes:	Route:	
	Distance:	Time:
	Weight:	Speed:
	Burn Cals:	Heart Rate:
	Weather:	Breathing:
	How I Felt:	
	Injuries:	
	Overall Thoughts:	

Thursday	Date:	Burns Target:
Notes:	Route:	
	Distance:	Time:
	Weight:	Speed:
	Burn Cals:	Heart Rate:
	Weather:	Breathing:
	How I Felt:	
	Injuries:	
	Overall Thoughts:	

Friday	Date:		Burns Target:	
Notes:	Route:			
	Distance:		Time:	
	Weight:		Speed:	
	Burn Cals:		Heart Rate:	
	Weather:		Breathing:	
	How I Felt:			
	Injuries:			
	Overall Thoughts:			

Saturday	Date:		Burns Target:	
Notes:	Route:			
	Distance:		Time:	
	Weight:		Speed:	
	Burn Cals:		Heart Rate:	
	Weather:		Breathing:	
	How I Felt:			
	Injuries:			
	Overall Thoughts:			

Sunday	Date:		Burns Target:	
Notes:	Route:			
	Distance:		Time:	
	Weight:		Speed:	
	Burn Cals:		Heart Rate:	
	Weather:		Breathing:	
	How I Felt:			
	Injuries:			
	Overall Thoughts:			

Weekly Review

Total Distance:		Weight loss:	
Average Speed:		Total Hours:	
Average Heart Rate:		Total Burns:	

Notes / Thoughts:

Year:_____ Month:_____ Week:_____ Weekly Goal:_____

Monday	Date:	Burns Target:
Notes:	Route:	
	Distance:	Time:
	Weight:	Speed:
	Burn Cals:	Heart Rate:
	Weather:	Breathing:
	How I Felt:	
	Injuries:	
	Overall Thoughts:	

Tuesday	Date:	Burns Target:
Notes:	Route:	
	Distance:	Time:
	Weight:	Speed:
	Burn Cals:	Heart Rate:
	Weather:	Breathing:
	How I Felt:	
	Injuries:	
	Overall Thoughts:	

Wednesday	Date:	Burns Target:
Notes:	Route:	
	Distance:	Time:
	Weight:	Speed:
	Burn Cals:	Heart Rate:
	Weather:	Breathing:
	How I Felt:	
	Injuries:	
	Overall Thoughts:	

Thursday	Date:	Burns Target:
Notes:	Route:	
	Distance:	Time:
	Weight:	Speed:
	Burn Cals:	Heart Rate:
	Weather:	Breathing:
	How I Felt:	
	Injuries:	
	Overall Thoughts:	

Friday	Date:		Burns Target:	
Notes:	Route:			
	Distance:		Time:	
	Weight:		Speed:	
	Burn Cals:		Heart Rate:	
	Weather:		Breathing:	
	How I Felt:			
	Injuries:			
	Overall Thoughts:			

Saturday	Date:		Burns Target:	
Notes:	Route:			
	Distance:		Time:	
	Weight:		Speed:	
	Burn Cals:		Heart Rate:	
	Weather:		Breathing:	
	How I Felt:			
	Injuries:			
	Overall Thoughts:			

Sunday	Date:		Burns Target:	
Notes:	Route:			
	Distance:		Time:	
	Weight:		Speed:	
	Burn Cals:		Heart Rate:	
	Weather:		Breathing:	
	How I Felt:			
	Injuries:			
	Overall Thoughts:			

Weekly Review			
Total Distance:		Weight loss:	
Average Speed:		Total Hours:	
Average Heart Rate:		Total Burns:	
Notes / Thoughts:			

Year: _____ Month: _____ Week: _____ Weekly Goal: _____

Monday	**Date:**		**Burns Target:**
Notes:	Route:		
	Distance:	Time:	
	Weight:	Speed:	
	Burn Cals:	Heart Rate:	
	Weather:	Breathing:	
	How I Felt:		
	Injuries:		
	Overall Thoughts:		

Tuesday	**Date:**		**Burns Target:**
Notes:	Route:		
	Distance:	Time:	
	Weight:	Speed:	
	Burn Cals:	Heart Rate:	
	Weather:	Breathing:	
	How I Felt:		
	Injuries:		
	Overall Thoughts:		

Wednesday	**Date:**		**Burns Target:**
Notes:	Route:		
	Distance:	Time:	
	Weight:	Speed:	
	Burn Cals:	Heart Rate:	
	Weather:	Breathing:	
	How I Felt:		
	Injuries:		
	Overall Thoughts:		

Thursday	**Date:**		**Burns Target:**
Notes:	Route:		
	Distance:	Time:	
	Weight:	Speed:	
	Burn Cals:	Heart Rate:	
	Weather:	Breathing:	
	How I Felt:		
	Injuries:		
	Overall Thoughts:		

Friday	Date:		Burns Target:	
Notes:	Route:			
	Distance:		Time:	
	Weight:		Speed:	
	Burn Cals:		Heart Rate:	
	Weather:		Breathing:	
	How I Felt:			
	Injuries:			
	Overall Thoughts:			

Saturday	Date:		Burns Target:	
Notes:	Route:			
	Distance:		Time:	
	Weight:		Speed:	
	Burn Cals:		Heart Rate:	
	Weather:		Breathing:	
	How I Felt:			
	Injuries:			
	Overall Thoughts:			

Sunday	Date:		Burns Target:	
Notes:	Route:			
	Distance:		Time:	
	Weight:		Speed:	
	Burn Cals:		Heart Rate:	
	Weather:		Breathing:	
	How I Felt:			
	Injuries:			
	Overall Thoughts:			

Weekly Review

Total Distance:		Weight loss:	
Average Speed:		Total Hours:	
Average Heart Rate:		Total Burns:	

Notes / Thoughts:

Year: _____ Month: _____ Week: _____ Weekly Goal: _____

Monday	Date:	Burns Target:
Notes:	Route:	
	Distance:	Time:
	Weight:	Speed:
	Burn Cals:	Heart Rate:
	Weather:	Breathing:
	How I Felt:	
	Injuries:	
	Overall Thoughts:	

Tuesday	Date:	Burns Target:
Notes:	Route:	
	Distance:	Time:
	Weight:	Speed:
	Burn Cals:	Heart Rate:
	Weather:	Breathing:
	How I Felt:	
	Injuries:	
	Overall Thoughts:	

Wednesday	Date:	Burns Target:
Notes:	Route:	
	Distance:	Time:
	Weight:	Speed:
	Burn Cals:	Heart Rate:
	Weather:	Breathing:
	How I Felt:	
	Injuries:	
	Overall Thoughts:	

Thursday	Date:	Burns Target:
Notes:	Route:	
	Distance:	Time:
	Weight:	Speed:
	Burn Cals:	Heart Rate:
	Weather:	Breathing:
	How I Felt:	
	Injuries:	
	Overall Thoughts:	

Friday	Date:	Burns Target:
Notes:	Route:	
	Distance:	Time:
	Weight:	Speed:
	Burn Cals:	Heart Rate:
	Weather:	Breathing:
	How I Felt:	
	Injuries:	
	Overall Thoughts:	

Saturday	Date:	Burns Target:
Notes:	Route:	
	Distance:	Time:
	Weight:	Speed:
	Burn Cals:	Heart Rate:
	Weather:	Breathing:
	How I Felt:	
	Injuries:	
	Overall Thoughts:	

Sunday	Date:	Burns Target:
Notes:	Route:	
	Distance:	Time:
	Weight:	Speed:
	Burn Cals:	Heart Rate:
	Weather:	Breathing:
	How I Felt:	
	Injuries:	
	Overall Thoughts:	

Weekly Review

Total Distance:		Weight loss:	
Average Speed:		Total Hours:	
Average Heart Rate:		Total Burns:	

Notes / Thoughts:

Year:_____ Month:_____ Week:_____ Weekly Goal:_____

Monday	Date:		Burns Target:	
Notes:	Route:			
	Distance:		Time:	
	Weight:		Speed:	
	Burn Cals:		Heart Rate:	
	Weather:		Breathing:	
	How I Felt:			
	Injuries:			
	Overall Thoughts:			

Tuesday	Date:		Burns Target:	
Notes:	Route:			
	Distance:		Time:	
	Weight:		Speed:	
	Burn Cals:		Heart Rate:	
	Weather:		Breathing:	
	How I Felt:			
	Injuries:			
	Overall Thoughts:			

Wednesday	Date:		Burns Target:	
Notes:	Route:			
	Distance:		Time:	
	Weight:		Speed:	
	Burn Cals:		Heart Rate:	
	Weather:		Breathing:	
	How I Felt:			
	Injuries:			
	Overall Thoughts:			

Thursday	Date:		Burns Target:	
Notes:	Route:			
	Distance:		Time:	
	Weight:		Speed:	
	Burn Cals:		Heart Rate:	
	Weather:		Breathing:	
	How I Felt:			
	Injuries:			
	Overall Thoughts:			

Friday	Date:		Burns Target:	
Notes:	Route:			
	Distance:		Time:	
	Weight:		Speed:	
	Burn Cals:		Heart Rate:	
	Weather:		Breathing:	
	How I Felt:			
	Injuries:			
	Overall Thoughts:			

Saturday	Date:		Burns Target:	
Notes:	Route:			
	Distance:		Time:	
	Weight:		Speed:	
	Burn Cals:		Heart Rate:	
	Weather:		Breathing:	
	How I Felt:			
	Injuries:			
	Overall Thoughts:			

Sunday	Date:		Burns Target:	
Notes:	Route:			
	Distance:		Time:	
	Weight:		Speed:	
	Burn Cals:		Heart Rate:	
	Weather:		Breathing:	
	How I Felt:			
	Injuries:			
	Overall Thoughts:			

Weekly Review

Total Distance:		Weight loss:	
Average Speed:		Total Hours:	
Average Heart Rate:		Total Burns:	

Notes / Thoughts:

Year: _____ Month: _____ Week: _____ Weekly Goal: _____

Monday	**Date:**	**Burns Target:**

Notes:

Route:	
Distance:	Time:
Weight:	Speed:
Burn Cals:	Heart Rate:
Weather:	Breathing:
How I Felt:	
Injuries:	
Overall Thoughts:	

Tuesday	**Date:**	**Burns Target:**

Notes:

Route:	
Distance:	Time:
Weight:	Speed:
Burn Cals:	Heart Rate:
Weather:	Breathing:
How I Felt:	
Injuries:	
Overall Thoughts:	

Wednesday	**Date:**	**Burns Target:**

Notes:

Route:	
Distance:	Time:
Weight:	Speed:
Burn Cals:	Heart Rate:
Weather:	Breathing:
How I Felt:	
Injuries:	
Overall Thoughts:	

Thursday	**Date:**	**Burns Target:**

Notes:

Route:	
Distance:	Time:
Weight:	Speed:
Burn Cals:	Heart Rate:
Weather:	Breathing:
How I Felt:	
Injuries:	
Overall Thoughts:	

Friday	Date:		Burns Target:	
Notes:	Route:			
	Distance:		Time:	
	Weight:		Speed:	
	Burn Cals:		Heart Rate:	
	Weather:		Breathing:	
	How I Felt:			
	Injuries:			
	Overall Thoughts:			

Saturday	Date:		Burns Target:	
Notes:	Route:			
	Distance:		Time:	
	Weight:		Speed:	
	Burn Cals:		Heart Rate:	
	Weather:		Breathing:	
	How I Felt:			
	Injuries:			
	Overall Thoughts:			

Sunday	Date:		Burns Target:	
Notes:	Route:			
	Distance:		Time:	
	Weight:		Speed:	
	Burn Cals:		Heart Rate:	
	Weather:		Breathing:	
	How I Felt:			
	Injuries:			
	Overall Thoughts:			

Weekly Review			
Total Distance:		Weight loss:	
Average Speed:		Total Hours:	
Average Heart Rate:		Total Burns:	
Notes / Thoughts:			

Year:_____ Month:_____ Week:_____ Weekly Goal:_____

Monday	Date:	Burns Target:
Notes:	Route:	
	Distance:	Time:
	Weight:	Speed:
	Burn Cals:	Heart Rate:
	Weather:	Breathing:
	How I Felt:	
	Injuries:	
	Overall Thoughts:	

Tuesday	Date:	Burns Target:
Notes:	Route:	
	Distance:	Time:
	Weight:	Speed:
	Burn Cals:	Heart Rate:
	Weather:	Breathing:
	How I Felt:	
	Injuries:	
	Overall Thoughts:	

Wednesday	Date:	Burns Target:
Notes:	Route:	
	Distance:	Time:
	Weight:	Speed:
	Burn Cals:	Heart Rate:
	Weather:	Breathing:
	How I Felt:	
	Injuries:	
	Overall Thoughts:	

Thursday	Date:	Burns Target:
Notes:	Route:	
	Distance:	Time:
	Weight:	Speed:
	Burn Cals:	Heart Rate:
	Weather:	Breathing:
	How I Felt:	
	Injuries:	
	Overall Thoughts:	

Friday	Date:		Burns Target:
Notes:	Route:		
	Distance:		Time:
	Weight:		Speed:
	Burn Cals:		Heart Rate:
	Weather:		Breathing:
	How I Felt:		
	Injuries:		
	Overall Thoughts:		

Saturday	Date:		Burns Target:
Notes:	Route:		
	Distance:		Time:
	Weight:		Speed:
	Burn Cals:		Heart Rate:
	Weather:		Breathing:
	How I Felt:		
	Injuries:		
	Overall Thoughts:		

Sunday	Date:		Burns Target:
Notes:	Route:		
	Distance:		Time:
	Weight:		Speed:
	Burn Cals:		Heart Rate:
	Weather:		Breathing:
	How I Felt:		
	Injuries:		
	Overall Thoughts:		

Weekly Review

Total Distance:		Weight loss:	
Average Speed:		Total Hours:	
Average Heart Rate:		Total Burns:	

Notes / Thoughts:

Year: .... Month: .... Week: .... Weekly Goal: ....

Monday	Date:		Burns Target:	
Notes:	Route:			
	Distance:		Time:	
	Weight:		Speed:	
	Burn Cals:		Heart Rate:	
	Weather:		Breathing:	
	How I Felt:			
	Injuries:			
	Overall Thoughts:			

Tuesday	Date:		Burns Target:	
Notes:	Route:			
	Distance:		Time:	
	Weight:		Speed:	
	Burn Cals:		Heart Rate:	
	Weather:		Breathing:	
	How I Felt:			
	Injuries:			
	Overall Thoughts:			

Wednesday	Date:		Burns Target:	
Notes:	Route:			
	Distance:		Time:	
	Weight:		Speed:	
	Burn Cals:		Heart Rate:	
	Weather:		Breathing:	
	How I Felt:			
	Injuries:			
	Overall Thoughts:			

Thursday	Date:		Burns Target:	
Notes:	Route:			
	Distance:		Time:	
	Weight:		Speed:	
	Burn Cals:		Heart Rate:	
	Weather:		Breathing:	
	How I Felt:			
	Injuries:			
	Overall Thoughts:			

Friday	Date:		Burns Target:	
Notes:	Route:			
	Distance:		Time:	
	Weight:		Speed:	
	Burn Cals:		Heart Rate:	
	Weather:		Breathing:	
	How I Felt:			
	Injuries:			
	Overall Thoughts:			

Saturday	Date:		Burns Target:	
Notes:	Route:			
	Distance:		Time:	
	Weight:		Speed:	
	Burn Cals:		Heart Rate:	
	Weather:		Breathing:	
	How I Felt:			
	Injuries:			
	Overall Thoughts:			

Sunday	Date:		Burns Target:	
Notes:	Route:			
	Distance:		Time:	
	Weight:		Speed:	
	Burn Cals:		Heart Rate:	
	Weather:		Breathing:	
	How I Felt:			
	Injuries:			
	Overall Thoughts:			

Weekly Review

Total Distance:		Weight loss:	
Average Speed:		Total Hours:	
Average Heart Rate:		Total Burns:	

Notes / Thoughts:

Year: .... Month: .... Week: .... Weekly Goal: ....

Monday	Date:	Burns Target:	
Notes:	Route:		
	Distance:	Time:	
	Weight:	Speed:	
	Burn Cals:	Heart Rate:	
	Weather:	Breathing:	
	How I Felt:		
	Injuries:		
	Overall Thoughts:		

Tuesday	Date:	Burns Target:	
Notes:	Route:		
	Distance:	Time:	
	Weight:	Speed:	
	Burn Cals:	Heart Rate:	
	Weather:	Breathing:	
	How I Felt:		
	Injuries:		
	Overall Thoughts:		

Wednesday	Date:	Burns Target:	
Notes:	Route:		
	Distance:	Time:	
	Weight:	Speed:	
	Burn Cals:	Heart Rate:	
	Weather:	Breathing:	
	How I Felt:		
	Injuries:		
	Overall Thoughts:		

Thursday	Date:	Burns Target:	
Notes:	Route:		
	Distance:	Time:	
	Weight:	Speed:	
	Burn Cals:	Heart Rate:	
	Weather:	Breathing:	
	How I Felt:		
	Injuries:		
	Overall Thoughts:		

Friday	Date:		Burns Target:	
Notes:	Route:			
	Distance:		Time:	
	Weight:		Speed:	
	Burn Cals:		Heart Rate:	
	Weather:		Breathing:	
	How I Felt:			
	Injuries:			
	Overall Thoughts:			

Saturday	Date:		Burns Target:	
Notes:	Route:			
	Distance:		Time:	
	Weight:		Speed:	
	Burn Cals:		Heart Rate:	
	Weather:		Breathing:	
	How I Felt:			
	Injuries:			
	Overall Thoughts:			

Sunday	Date:		Burns Target:	
Notes:	Route:			
	Distance:		Time:	
	Weight:		Speed:	
	Burn Cals:		Heart Rate:	
	Weather:		Breathing:	
	How I Felt:			
	Injuries:			
	Overall Thoughts:			

Weekly Review

Total Distance:		Weight loss:	
Average Speed:		Total Hours:	
Average Heart Rate:		Total Burns:	

Notes / Thoughts:

Year:............ Month:............ Week:............ Weekly Goal:..........

Monday	Date:		Burns Target:	
Notes:	Route:			
	Distance:		Time:	
	Weight:		Speed:	
	Burn Cals:		Heart Rate:	
	Weather:		Breathing:	
	How I Felt:			
	Injuries:			
	Overall Thoughts:			

Tuesday	Date:		Burns Target:	
Notes:	Route:			
	Distance:		Time:	
	Weight:		Speed:	
	Burn Cals:		Heart Rate:	
	Weather:		Breathing:	
	How I Felt:			
	Injuries:			
	Overall Thoughts:			

Wednesday	Date:		Burns Target:	
Notes:	Route:			
	Distance:		Time:	
	Weight:		Speed:	
	Burn Cals:		Heart Rate:	
	Weather:		Breathing:	
	How I Felt:			
	Injuries:			
	Overall Thoughts:			

Thursday	Date:		Burns Target:	
Notes:	Route:			
	Distance:		Time:	
	Weight:		Speed:	
	Burn Cals:		Heart Rate:	
	Weather:		Breathing:	
	How I Felt:			
	Injuries:			
	Overall Thoughts:			

Friday	Date:		Burns Target:	
Notes:	Route:			
	Distance:		Time:	
	Weight:		Speed:	
	Burn Cals:		Heart Rate:	
	Weather:		Breathing:	
	How I Felt:			
	Injuries:			
	Overall Thoughts:			

Saturday	Date:		Burns Target:	
Notes:	Route:			
	Distance:		Time:	
	Weight:		Speed:	
	Burn Cals:		Heart Rate:	
	Weather:		Breathing:	
	How I Felt:			
	Injuries:			
	Overall Thoughts:			

Sunday	Date:		Burns Target:	
Notes:	Route:			
	Distance:		Time:	
	Weight:		Speed:	
	Burn Cals:		Heart Rate:	
	Weather:		Breathing:	
	How I Felt:			
	Injuries:			
	Overall Thoughts:			

Weekly Review

Total Distance:		Weight loss:	
Average Speed:		Total Hours:	
Average Heart Rate:		Total Burns:	

Notes / Thoughts:

Year:_____ Month:_____ Week:_____ Weekly Goal:_____

Monday	Date:	Burns Target:
Notes:	Route:	
	Distance:	Time:
	Weight:	Speed:
	Burn Cals:	Heart Rate:
	Weather:	Breathing:
	How I Felt:	
	Injuries:	
	Overall Thoughts:	

Tuesday	Date:	Burns Target:
Notes:	Route:	
	Distance:	Time:
	Weight:	Speed:
	Burn Cals:	Heart Rate:
	Weather:	Breathing:
	How I Felt:	
	Injuries:	
	Overall Thoughts:	

Wednesday	Date:	Burns Target:
Notes:	Route:	
	Distance:	Time:
	Weight:	Speed:
	Burn Cals:	Heart Rate:
	Weather:	Breathing:
	How I Felt:	
	Injuries:	
	Overall Thoughts:	

Thursday	Date:	Burns Target:
Notes:	Route:	
	Distance:	Time:
	Weight:	Speed:
	Burn Cals:	Heart Rate:
	Weather:	Breathing:
	How I Felt:	
	Injuries:	
	Overall Thoughts:	

Friday	Date:		Burns Target:
Notes:	Route:		
	Distance:	Time:	
	Weight:	Speed:	
	Burn Cals:	Heart Rate:	
	Weather:	Breathing:	
	How I Felt:		
	Injuries:		
	Overall Thoughts:		

Saturday	Date:		Burns Target:
Notes:	Route:		
	Distance:	Time:	
	Weight:	Speed:	
	Burn Cals:	Heart Rate:	
	Weather:	Breathing:	
	How I Felt:		
	Injuries:		
	Overall Thoughts:		

Sunday	Date:		Burns Target:
Notes:	Route:		
	Distance:	Time:	
	Weight:	Speed:	
	Burn Cals:	Heart Rate:	
	Weather:	Breathing:	
	How I Felt:		
	Injuries:		
	Overall Thoughts:		

Weekly Review

Total Distance:		Weight loss:	
Average Speed:		Total Hours:	
Average Heart Rate:		Total Burns:	
Notes / Thoughts:			

Year: _____ Month: _____ Week: _____ Weekly Goal: _____

Monday	Date:	Burns Target:
Notes:	Route:	
	Distance:	Time:
	Weight:	Speed:
	Burn Cals:	Heart Rate:
	Weather:	Breathing:
	How I Felt:	
	Injuries:	
	Overall Thoughts:	

Tuesday	Date:	Burns Target:
Notes:	Route:	
	Distance:	Time:
	Weight:	Speed:
	Burn Cals:	Heart Rate:
	Weather:	Breathing:
	How I Felt:	
	Injuries:	
	Overall Thoughts:	

Wednesday	Date:	Burns Target:
Notes:	Route:	
	Distance:	Time:
	Weight:	Speed:
	Burn Cals:	Heart Rate:
	Weather:	Breathing:
	How I Felt:	
	Injuries:	
	Overall Thoughts:	

Thursday	Date:	Burns Target:
Notes:	Route:	
	Distance:	Time:
	Weight:	Speed:
	Burn Cals:	Heart Rate:
	Weather:	Breathing:
	How I Felt:	
	Injuries:	
	Overall Thoughts:	

Friday	Date:		Burns Target:	
Notes:	Route:			
	Distance:		Time:	
	Weight:		Speed:	
	Burn Cals:		Heart Rate:	
	Weather:		Breathing:	
	How I Felt:			
	Injuries:			
	Overall Thoughts:			

Saturday	Date:		Burns Target:	
Notes:	Route:			
	Distance:		Time:	
	Weight:		Speed:	
	Burn Cals:		Heart Rate:	
	Weather:		Breathing:	
	How I Felt:			
	Injuries:			
	Overall Thoughts:			

Sunday	Date:		Burns Target:	
Notes:	Route:			
	Distance:		Time:	
	Weight:		Speed:	
	Burn Cals:		Heart Rate:	
	Weather:		Breathing:	
	How I Felt:			
	Injuries:			
	Overall Thoughts:			

Weekly Review

Total Distance:		Weight loss:	
Average Speed:		Total Hours:	
Average Heart Rate:		Total Burns:	

Notes / Thoughts:

Year: _____ Month: _____ Week: _____ Weekly Goal: _____

Monday	Date:	Burns Target:
Notes:	Route:	
	Distance:	Time:
	Weight:	Speed:
	Burn Cals:	Heart Rate:
	Weather:	Breathing:
	How I Felt:	
	Injuries:	
	Overall Thoughts:	

Tuesday	Date:	Burns Target:
Notes:	Route:	
	Distance:	Time:
	Weight:	Speed:
	Burn Cals:	Heart Rate:
	Weather:	Breathing:
	How I Felt:	
	Injuries:	
	Overall Thoughts:	

Wednesday	Date:	Burns Target:
Notes:	Route:	
	Distance:	Time:
	Weight:	Speed:
	Burn Cals:	Heart Rate:
	Weather:	Breathing:
	How I Felt:	
	Injuries:	
	Overall Thoughts:	

Thursday	Date:	Burns Target:
Notes:	Route:	
	Distance:	Time:
	Weight:	Speed:
	Burn Cals:	Heart Rate:
	Weather:	Breathing:
	How I Felt:	
	Injuries:	
	Overall Thoughts:	

Friday	Date:		Burns Target:
Notes:	Route:		
	Distance:	Time:	
	Weight:	Speed:	
	Burn Cals:	Heart Rate:	
	Weather:	Breathing:	
	How I Felt:		
	Injuries:		
	Overall Thoughts:		

Saturday	Date:		Burns Target:
Notes:	Route:		
	Distance:	Time:	
	Weight:	Speed:	
	Burn Cals:	Heart Rate:	
	Weather:	Breathing:	
	How I Felt:		
	Injuries:		
	Overall Thoughts:		

Sunday	Date:		Burns Target:
Notes:	Route:		
	Distance:	Time:	
	Weight:	Speed:	
	Burn Cals:	Heart Rate:	
	Weather:	Breathing:	
	How I Felt:		
	Injuries:		
	Overall Thoughts:		

Weekly Review

Total Distance:		Weight loss:	
Average Speed:		Total Hours:	
Average Heart Rate:		Total Burns:	

Notes / Thoughts:

Year:............ Month:............ Week:............ Weekly Goal:.........

Monday	Date:		Burns Target:	
Notes:	Route:			
	Distance:		Time:	
	Weight:		Speed:	
	Burn Cals:		Heart Rate:	
	Weather:		Breathing:	
	How I Felt:			
	Injuries:			
	Overall Thoughts:			

Tuesday	Date:		Burns Target:	
Notes:	Route:			
	Distance:		Time:	
	Weight:		Speed:	
	Burn Cals:		Heart Rate:	
	Weather:		Breathing:	
	How I Felt:			
	Injuries:			
	Overall Thoughts:			

Wednesday	Date:		Burns Target:	
Notes:	Route:			
	Distance:		Time:	
	Weight:		Speed:	
	Burn Cals:		Heart Rate:	
	Weather:		Breathing:	
	How I Felt:			
	Injuries:			
	Overall Thoughts:			

Thursday	Date:		Burns Target:	
Notes:	Route:			
	Distance:		Time:	
	Weight:		Speed:	
	Burn Cals:		Heart Rate:	
	Weather:		Breathing:	
	How I Felt:			
	Injuries:			
	Overall Thoughts:			

Friday	Date:		Burns Target:	
Notes:	Route:			
	Distance:		Time:	
	Weight:		Speed:	
	Burn Cals:		Heart Rate:	
	Weather:		Breathing:	
	How I Felt:			
	Injuries:			
	Overall Thoughts:			

Saturday	Date:		Burns Target:	
Notes:	Route:			
	Distance:		Time:	
	Weight:		Speed:	
	Burn Cals:		Heart Rate:	
	Weather:		Breathing:	
	How I Felt:			
	Injuries:			
	Overall Thoughts:			

Sunday	Date:		Burns Target:	
Notes:	Route:			
	Distance:		Time:	
	Weight:		Speed:	
	Burn Cals:		Heart Rate:	
	Weather:		Breathing:	
	How I Felt:			
	Injuries:			
	Overall Thoughts:			

Weekly Review

Total Distance:		Weight loss:	
Average Speed:		Total Hours:	
Average Heart Rate:		Total Burns:	

Notes / Thoughts:

Year:_____ Month:_____ Week:_____ Weekly Goal:_____

Monday	Date:	Burns Target:
Notes:	Route:	
	Distance:	Time:
	Weight:	Speed:
	Burn Cals:	Heart Rate:
	Weather:	Breathing:
	How I Felt:	
	Injuries:	
	Overall Thoughts:	

Tuesday	Date:	Burns Target:
Notes:	Route:	
	Distance:	Time:
	Weight:	Speed:
	Burn Cals:	Heart Rate:
	Weather:	Breathing:
	How I Felt:	
	Injuries:	
	Overall Thoughts:	

Wednesday	Date:	Burns Target:
Notes:	Route:	
	Distance:	Time:
	Weight:	Speed:
	Burn Cals:	Heart Rate:
	Weather:	Breathing:
	How I Felt:	
	Injuries:	
	Overall Thoughts:	

Thursday	Date:	Burns Target:
Notes:	Route:	
	Distance:	Time:
	Weight:	Speed:
	Burn Cals:	Heart Rate:
	Weather:	Breathing:
	How I Felt:	
	Injuries:	
	Overall Thoughts:	

Friday	Date:		Burns Target:	
Notes:	Route:			
	Distance:		Time:	
	Weight:		Speed:	
	Burn Cals:		Heart Rate:	
	Weather:		Breathing:	
	How I Felt:			
	Injuries:			
	Overall Thoughts:			

Saturday	Date:		Burns Target:	
Notes:	Route:			
	Distance:		Time:	
	Weight:		Speed:	
	Burn Cals:		Heart Rate:	
	Weather:		Breathing:	
	How I Felt:			
	Injuries:			
	Overall Thoughts:			

Sunday	Date:		Burns Target:	
Notes:	Route:			
	Distance:		Time:	
	Weight:		Speed:	
	Burn Cals:		Heart Rate:	
	Weather:		Breathing:	
	How I Felt:			
	Injuries:			
	Overall Thoughts:			

Weekly Review

Total Distance:		Weight loss:	
Average Speed:		Total Hours:	
Average Heart Rate:		Total Burns:	

Notes / Thoughts:

Year: .... Month: .... Week: .... Weekly Goal: ....

Monday	Date:		Burns Target:	
Notes:	Route:			
	Distance:		Time:	
	Weight:		Speed:	
	Burn Cals:		Heart Rate:	
	Weather:		Breathing:	
	How I Felt:			
	Injuries:			
	Overall Thoughts:			

Tuesday	Date:		Burns Target:	
Notes:	Route:			
	Distance:		Time:	
	Weight:		Speed:	
	Burn Cals:		Heart Rate:	
	Weather:		Breathing:	
	How I Felt:			
	Injuries:			
	Overall Thoughts:			

Wednesday	Date:		Burns Target:	
Notes:	Route:			
	Distance:		Time:	
	Weight:		Speed:	
	Burn Cals:		Heart Rate:	
	Weather:		Breathing:	
	How I Felt:			
	Injuries:			
	Overall Thoughts:			

Thursday	Date:		Burns Target:	
Notes:	Route:			
	Distance:		Time:	
	Weight:		Speed:	
	Burn Cals:		Heart Rate:	
	Weather:		Breathing:	
	How I Felt:			
	Injuries:			
	Overall Thoughts:			

Friday	Date:	Burns Target:	
Notes:	Route:		
	Distance:	Time:	
	Weight:	Speed:	
	Burn Cals:	Heart Rate:	
	Weather:	Breathing:	
	How I Felt:		
	Injuries:		
	Overall Thoughts:		

Saturday	Date:	Burns Target:	
Notes:	Route:		
	Distance:	Time:	
	Weight:	Speed:	
	Burn Cals:	Heart Rate:	
	Weather:	Breathing:	
	How I Felt:		
	Injuries:		
	Overall Thoughts:		

Sunday	Date:	Burns Target:	
Notes:	Route:		
	Distance:	Time:	
	Weight:	Speed:	
	Burn Cals:	Heart Rate:	
	Weather:	Breathing:	
	How I Felt:		
	Injuries:		
	Overall Thoughts:		

Weekly Review

Total Distance:		Weight loss:	
Average Speed:		Total Hours:	
Average Heart Rate:		Total Burns:	

Notes / Thoughts:

Year: _____ Month: _____ Week: _____ Weekly Goal: _____

Monday	Date:	Burns Target:
Notes:	Route:	
	Distance:	Time:
	Weight:	Speed:
	Burn Cals:	Heart Rate:
	Weather:	Breathing:
	How I Felt:	
	Injuries:	
	Overall Thoughts:	

Tuesday	Date:	Burns Target:
Notes:	Route:	
	Distance:	Time:
	Weight:	Speed:
	Burn Cals:	Heart Rate:
	Weather:	Breathing:
	How I Felt:	
	Injuries:	
	Overall Thoughts:	

Wednesday	Date:	Burns Target:
Notes:	Route:	
	Distance:	Time:
	Weight:	Speed:
	Burn Cals:	Heart Rate:
	Weather:	Breathing:
	How I Felt:	
	Injuries:	
	Overall Thoughts:	

Thursday	Date:	Burns Target:
Notes:	Route:	
	Distance:	Time:
	Weight:	Speed:
	Burn Cals:	Heart Rate:
	Weather:	Breathing:
	How I Felt:	
	Injuries:	
	Overall Thoughts:	

Friday	Date:		Burns Target:
Notes:	Route:		
	Distance:		Time:
	Weight:		Speed:
	Burn Cals:		Heart Rate:
	Weather:		Breathing:
	How I Felt:		
	Injuries:		
	Overall Thoughts:		

Saturday	Date:		Burns Target:
Notes:	Route:		
	Distance:		Time:
	Weight:		Speed:
	Burn Cals:		Heart Rate:
	Weather:		Breathing:
	How I Felt:		
	Injuries:		
	Overall Thoughts:		

Sunday	Date:		Burns Target:
Notes:	Route:		
	Distance:		Time:
	Weight:		Speed:
	Burn Cals:		Heart Rate:
	Weather:		Breathing:
	How I Felt:		
	Injuries:		
	Overall Thoughts:		

Weekly Review

Total Distance:		Weight loss:	
Average Speed:		Total Hours:	
Average Heart Rate:		Total Burns:	

Notes / Thoughts:

Year: .... Month: .... Week: .... Weekly Goal: ....

Monday	Date:		**Burns Target:**	
Notes:	Route:			
	Distance:		Time:	
	Weight:		Speed:	
	Burn Cals:		Heart Rate:	
	Weather:		Breathing:	
	How I Felt:			
	Injuries:			
	Overall Thoughts:			

Tuesday	Date:		**Burns Target:**	
Notes:	Route:			
	Distance:		Time:	
	Weight:		Speed:	
	Burn Cals:		Heart Rate:	
	Weather:		Breathing:	
	How I Felt:			
	Injuries:			
	Overall Thoughts:			

Wednesday	Date:		**Burns Target:**	
Notes:	Route:			
	Distance:		Time:	
	Weight:		Speed:	
	Burn Cals:		Heart Rate:	
	Weather:		Breathing:	
	How I Felt:			
	Injuries:			
	Overall Thoughts:			

Thursday	Date:		**Burns Target:**	
Notes:	Route:			
	Distance:		Time:	
	Weight:		Speed:	
	Burn Cals:		Heart Rate:	
	Weather:		Breathing:	
	How I Felt:			
	Injuries:			
	Overall Thoughts:			

Friday	Date:		Burns Target:	
Notes:	Route:			
	Distance:		Time:	
	Weight:		Speed:	
	Burn Cals:		Heart Rate:	
	Weather:		Breathing:	
	How I Felt:			
	Injuries:			
	Overall Thoughts:			

Saturday	Date:		Burns Target:	
Notes:	Route:			
	Distance:		Time:	
	Weight:		Speed:	
	Burn Cals:		Heart Rate:	
	Weather:		Breathing:	
	How I Felt:			
	Injuries:			
	Overall Thoughts:			

Sunday	Date:		Burns Target:	
Notes:	Route:			
	Distance:		Time:	
	Weight:		Speed:	
	Burn Cals:		Heart Rate:	
	Weather:		Breathing:	
	How I Felt:			
	Injuries:			
	Overall Thoughts:			

Weekly Review

Total Distance:		Weight loss:	
Average Speed:		Total Hours:	
Average Heart Rate:		Total Burns:	

Notes / Thoughts:

Year: .... Month: .... Week: .... Weekly Goal: ....

Monday	Date:		Burns Target:	
Notes:	Route:			
	Distance:		Time:	
	Weight:		Speed:	
	Burn Cals:		Heart Rate:	
	Weather:		Breathing:	
	How I Felt:			
	Injuries:			
	Overall Thoughts:			

Tuesday	Date:		Burns Target:	
Notes:	Route:			
	Distance:		Time:	
	Weight:		Speed:	
	Burn Cals:		Heart Rate:	
	Weather:		Breathing:	
	How I Felt:			
	Injuries:			
	Overall Thoughts:			

Wednesday	Date:		Burns Target:	
Notes:	Route:			
	Distance:		Time:	
	Weight:		Speed:	
	Burn Cals:		Heart Rate:	
	Weather:		Breathing:	
	How I Felt:			
	Injuries:			
	Overall Thoughts:			

Thursday	Date:		Burns Target:	
Notes:	Route:			
	Distance:		Time:	
	Weight:		Speed:	
	Burn Cals:		Heart Rate:	
	Weather:		Breathing:	
	How I Felt:			
	Injuries:			
	Overall Thoughts:			

Friday	Date:	Burns Target:	
Notes:	Route:		
	Distance:	Time:	
	Weight:	Speed:	
	Burn Cals:	Heart Rate:	
	Weather:	Breathing:	
	How I Felt:		
	Injuries:		
	Overall Thoughts:		

Saturday	Date:	Burns Target:	
Notes:	Route:		
	Distance:	Time:	
	Weight:	Speed:	
	Burn Cals:	Heart Rate:	
	Weather:	Breathing:	
	How I Felt:		
	Injuries:		
	Overall Thoughts:		

Sunday	Date:	Burns Target:	
Notes:	Route:		
	Distance:	Time:	
	Weight:	Speed:	
	Burn Cals:	Heart Rate:	
	Weather:	Breathing:	
	How I Felt:		
	Injuries:		
	Overall Thoughts:		

Weekly Review

Total Distance:		Weight loss:	
Average Speed:		Total Hours:	
Average Heart Rate:		Total Burns:	

Notes / Thoughts:

Year:............ Month:............ Week:............ Weekly Goal:.........

Monday	Date:	Burns Target:		
Notes:	Route:			
	Distance:		Time:	
	Weight:		Speed:	
	Burn Cals:		Heart Rate:	
	Weather:		Breathing:	
	How I Felt:			
	Injuries:			
	Overall Thoughts:			

Tuesday	Date:	Burns Target:		
Notes:	Route:			
	Distance:		Time:	
	Weight:		Speed:	
	Burn Cals:		Heart Rate:	
	Weather:		Breathing:	
	How I Felt:			
	Injuries:			
	Overall Thoughts:			

Wednesday	Date:	Burns Target:		
Notes:	Route:			
	Distance:		Time:	
	Weight:		Speed:	
	Burn Cals:		Heart Rate:	
	Weather:		Breathing:	
	How I Felt:			
	Injuries:			
	Overall Thoughts:			

Thursday	Date:	Burns Target:		
Notes:	Route:			
	Distance:		Time:	
	Weight:		Speed:	
	Burn Cals:		Heart Rate:	
	Weather:		Breathing:	
	How I Felt:			
	Injuries:			
	Overall Thoughts:			

Friday	Date:		Burns Target:
Notes:	Route:		
	Distance:		Time:
	Weight:		Speed:
	Burn Cals:		Heart Rate:
	Weather:		Breathing:
	How I Felt:		
	Injuries:		
	Overall Thoughts:		

Saturday	Date:		Burns Target:
Notes:	Route:		
	Distance:		Time:
	Weight:		Speed:
	Burn Cals:		Heart Rate:
	Weather:		Breathing:
	How I Felt:		
	Injuries:		
	Overall Thoughts:		

Sunday	Date:		Burns Target:
Notes:	Route:		
	Distance:		Time:
	Weight:		Speed:
	Burn Cals:		Heart Rate:
	Weather:		Breathing:
	How I Felt:		
	Injuries:		
	Overall Thoughts:		

Weekly Review

Total Distance:		Weight loss:	
Average Speed:		Total Hours:	
Average Heart Rate:		Total Burns:	

Notes / Thoughts:

Year: _____ Month: _____ Week: _____ Weekly Goal: _____

Monday	Date:	Burns Target:
Notes:	Route:	
	Distance:	Time:
	Weight:	Speed:
	Burn Cals:	Heart Rate:
	Weather:	Breathing:
	How I Felt:	
	Injuries:	
	Overall Thoughts:	

Tuesday	Date:	Burns Target:
Notes:	Route:	
	Distance:	Time:
	Weight:	Speed:
	Burn Cals:	Heart Rate:
	Weather:	Breathing:
	How I Felt:	
	Injuries:	
	Overall Thoughts:	

Wednesday	Date:	Burns Target:
Notes:	Route:	
	Distance:	Time:
	Weight:	Speed:
	Burn Cals:	Heart Rate:
	Weather:	Breathing:
	How I Felt:	
	Injuries:	
	Overall Thoughts:	

Thursday	Date:	Burns Target:
Notes:	Route:	
	Distance:	Time:
	Weight:	Speed:
	Burn Cals:	Heart Rate:
	Weather:	Breathing:
	How I Felt:	
	Injuries:	
	Overall Thoughts:	

Friday	Date:		Burns Target:	
Notes:	Route:			
	Distance:		Time:	
	Weight:		Speed:	
	Burn Cals:		Heart Rate:	
	Weather:		Breathing:	
	How I Felt:			
	Injuries:			
	Overall Thoughts:			

Saturday	Date:		Burns Target:	
Notes:	Route:			
	Distance:		Time:	
	Weight:		Speed:	
	Burn Cals:		Heart Rate:	
	Weather:		Breathing:	
	How I Felt:			
	Injuries:			
	Overall Thoughts:			

Sunday	Date:		Burns Target:	
Notes:	Route:			
	Distance:		Time:	
	Weight:		Speed:	
	Burn Cals:		Heart Rate:	
	Weather:		Breathing:	
	How I Felt:			
	Injuries:			
	Overall Thoughts:			

Weekly Review

Total Distance:		Weight loss:	
Average Speed:		Total Hours:	
Average Heart Rate:		Total Burns:	

Notes / Thoughts:

Year:_____ Month:_____ Week:_____ Weekly Goal:_____

Monday	Date:		Burns Target:
Notes:	Route:		
	Distance:		Time:
	Weight:		Speed:
	Burn Cals:		Heart Rate:
	Weather:		Breathing:
	How I Felt:		
	Injuries:		
	Overall Thoughts:		

Tuesday	Date:		Burns Target:
Notes:	Route:		
	Distance:		Time:
	Weight:		Speed:
	Burn Cals:		Heart Rate:
	Weather:		Breathing:
	How I Felt:		
	Injuries:		
	Overall Thoughts:		

Wednesday	Date:		Burns Target:
Notes:	Route:		
	Distance:		Time:
	Weight:		Speed:
	Burn Cals:		Heart Rate:
	Weather:		Breathing:
	How I Felt:		
	Injuries:		
	Overall Thoughts:		

Thursday	Date:		Burns Target:
Notes:	Route:		
	Distance:		Time:
	Weight:		Speed:
	Burn Cals:		Heart Rate:
	Weather:		Breathing:
	How I Felt:		
	Injuries:		
	Overall Thoughts:		

Friday

Date: **Burns Target:**

Notes:

Route:	
Distance:	Time:
Weight:	Speed:
Burn Cals:	Heart Rate:
Weather:	Breathing:
How I Felt:	
Injuries:	
Overall Thoughts:	

Saturday

Date: **Burns Target:**

Notes:

Route:	
Distance:	Time:
Weight:	Speed:
Burn Cals:	Heart Rate:
Weather:	Breathing:
How I Felt:	
Injuries:	
Overall Thoughts:	

Sunday

Date: **Burns Target:**

Notes:

Route:	
Distance:	Time:
Weight:	Speed:
Burn Cals:	Heart Rate:
Weather:	Breathing:
How I Felt:	
Injuries:	
Overall Thoughts:	

Weekly Review

Total Distance:		Weight loss:	
Average Speed:		Total Hours:	
Average Heart Rate:		Total Burns:	

Notes / Thoughts:

Year:_____ Month:_____ Week:_____ Weekly Goal:_____

Monday	**Date:**		**Burns Target:**	
Notes:	Route:			
	Distance:		Time:	
	Weight:		Speed:	
	Burn Cals:		Heart Rate:	
	Weather:		Breathing:	
	How I Felt:			
	Injuries:			
	Overall Thoughts:			

Tuesday	**Date:**		**Burns Target:**	
Notes:	Route:			
	Distance:		Time:	
	Weight:		Speed:	
	Burn Cals:		Heart Rate:	
	Weather:		Breathing:	
	How I Felt:			
	Injuries:			
	Overall Thoughts:			

Wednesday	**Date:**		**Burns Target:**	
Notes:	Route:			
	Distance:		Time:	
	Weight:		Speed:	
	Burn Cals:		Heart Rate:	
	Weather:		Breathing:	
	How I Felt:			
	Injuries:			
	Overall Thoughts:			

Thursday	**Date:**		**Burns Target:**	
Notes:	Route:			
	Distance:		Time:	
	Weight:		Speed:	
	Burn Cals:		Heart Rate:	
	Weather:		Breathing:	
	How I Felt:			
	Injuries:			
	Overall Thoughts:			

Friday	Date:		Burns Target:
Notes:	Route:		
	Distance:		Time:
	Weight:		Speed:
	Burn Cals:		Heart Rate:
	Weather:		Breathing:
	How I Felt:		
	Injuries:		
	Overall Thoughts:		

Saturday	Date:		Burns Target:
Notes:	Route:		
	Distance:		Time:
	Weight:		Speed:
	Burn Cals:		Heart Rate:
	Weather:		Breathing:
	How I Felt:		
	Injuries:		
	Overall Thoughts:		

Sunday	Date:		Burns Target:
Notes:	Route:		
	Distance:		Time:
	Weight:		Speed:
	Burn Cals:		Heart Rate:
	Weather:		Breathing:
	How I Felt:		
	Injuries:		
	Overall Thoughts:		

Weekly Review

Total Distance:		Weight loss:	
Average Speed:		Total Hours:	
Average Heart Rate:		Total Burns:	

Notes / Thoughts:

Year:_____ Month:_____ Week:_____ Weekly Goal:_____

Monday	**Date:**	**Burns Target:**
Notes:	Route:	
	Distance:	Time:
	Weight:	Speed:
	Burn Cals:	Heart Rate:
	Weather:	Breathing:
	How I Felt:	
	Injuries:	
	Overall Thoughts:	

Tuesday	**Date:**	**Burns Target:**
Notes:	Route:	
	Distance:	Time:
	Weight:	Speed:
	Burn Cals:	Heart Rate:
	Weather:	Breathing:
	How I Felt:	
	Injuries:	
	Overall Thoughts:	

Wednesday	**Date:**	**Burns Target:**
Notes:	Route:	
	Distance:	Time:
	Weight:	Speed:
	Burn Cals:	Heart Rate:
	Weather:	Breathing:
	How I Felt:	
	Injuries:	
	Overall Thoughts:	

Thursday	**Date:**	**Burns Target:**
Notes:	Route:	
	Distance:	Time:
	Weight:	Speed:
	Burn Cals:	Heart Rate:
	Weather:	Breathing:
	How I Felt:	
	Injuries:	
	Overall Thoughts:	

Friday	Date:	Burns Target:	
Notes:	Route:		
	Distance:	Time:	
	Weight:	Speed:	
	Burn Cals:	Heart Rate:	
	Weather:	Breathing:	
	How I Felt:		
	Injuries:		
	Overall Thoughts:		

Saturday	Date:	Burns Target:	
Notes:	Route:		
	Distance:	Time:	
	Weight:	Speed:	
	Burn Cals:	Heart Rate:	
	Weather:	Breathing:	
	How I Felt:		
	Injuries:		
	Overall Thoughts:		

Sunday	Date:	Burns Target:	
Notes:	Route:		
	Distance:	Time:	
	Weight:	Speed:	
	Burn Cals:	Heart Rate:	
	Weather:	Breathing:	
	How I Felt:		
	Injuries:		
	Overall Thoughts:		

Weekly Review

Total Distance:		Weight loss:	
Average Speed:		Total Hours:	
Average Heart Rate:		Total Burns:	
Notes / Thoughts:			

Year:.............. Month:.............. Week:.............. Weekly Goal:..........

Monday	**Date:**	**Burns Target:**
Notes:	Route:	
	Distance:	Time:
	Weight:	Speed:
	Burn Cals:	Heart Rate:
	Weather:	Breathing:
	How I Felt:	
	Injuries:	
	Overall Thoughts:	

Tuesday	**Date:**	**Burns Target:**
Notes:	Route:	
	Distance:	Time:
	Weight:	Speed:
	Burn Cals:	Heart Rate:
	Weather:	Breathing:
	How I Felt:	
	Injuries:	
	Overall Thoughts:	

Wednesday	**Date:**	**Burns Target:**
Notes:	Route:	
	Distance:	Time:
	Weight:	Speed:
	Burn Cals:	Heart Rate:
	Weather:	Breathing:
	How I Felt:	
	Injuries:	
	Overall Thoughts:	

Thursday	**Date:**	**Burns Target:**
Notes:	Route:	
	Distance:	Time:
	Weight:	Speed:
	Burn Cals:	Heart Rate:
	Weather:	Breathing:
	How I Felt:	
	Injuries:	
	Overall Thoughts:	

Friday	Date:		Burns Target:	
Notes:	Route:			
	Distance:		Time:	
	Weight:		Speed:	
	Burn Cals:		Heart Rate:	
	Weather:		Breathing:	
	How I Felt:			
	Injuries:			
	Overall Thoughts:			

Saturday	Date:		Burns Target:	
Notes:	Route:			
	Distance:		Time:	
	Weight:		Speed:	
	Burn Cals:		Heart Rate:	
	Weather:		Breathing:	
	How I Felt:			
	Injuries:			
	Overall Thoughts:			

Sunday	Date:		Burns Target:	
Notes:	Route:			
	Distance:		Time:	
	Weight:		Speed:	
	Burn Cals:		Heart Rate:	
	Weather:		Breathing:	
	How I Felt:			
	Injuries:			
	Overall Thoughts:			

Weekly Review

Total Distance:		Weight loss:	
Average Speed:		Total Hours:	
Average Heart Rate:		Total Burns:	

Notes / Thoughts:

Year: .... Month: .... Week: .... Weekly Goal: ....

Monday	Date:		Burns Target:	
Notes:	Route:			
	Distance:		Time:	
	Weight:		Speed:	
	Burn Cals:		Heart Rate:	
	Weather:		Breathing:	
	How I Felt:			
	Injuries:			
	Overall Thoughts:			

Tuesday	Date:		Burns Target:	
Notes:	Route:			
	Distance:		Time:	
	Weight:		Speed:	
	Burn Cals:		Heart Rate:	
	Weather:		Breathing:	
	How I Felt:			
	Injuries:			
	Overall Thoughts:			

Wednesday	Date:		Burns Target:	
Notes:	Route:			
	Distance:		Time:	
	Weight:		Speed:	
	Burn Cals:		Heart Rate:	
	Weather:		Breathing:	
	How I Felt:			
	Injuries:			
	Overall Thoughts:			

Thursday	Date:		Burns Target:	
Notes:	Route:			
	Distance:		Time:	
	Weight:		Speed:	
	Burn Cals:		Heart Rate:	
	Weather:		Breathing:	
	How I Felt:			
	Injuries:			
	Overall Thoughts:			

Friday	Date:		Burns Target:
Notes:	Route:		
	Distance:		Time:
	Weight:		Speed:
	Burn Cals:		Heart Rate:
	Weather:		Breathing:
	How I Felt:		
	Injuries:		
	Overall Thoughts:		

Saturday	Date:		Burns Target:
Notes:	Route:		
	Distance:		Time:
	Weight:		Speed:
	Burn Cals:		Heart Rate:
	Weather:		Breathing:
	How I Felt:		
	Injuries:		
	Overall Thoughts:		

Sunday	Date:		Burns Target:
Notes:	Route:		
	Distance:		Time:
	Weight:		Speed:
	Burn Cals:		Heart Rate:
	Weather:		Breathing:
	How I Felt:		
	Injuries:		
	Overall Thoughts:		

Weekly Review

Total Distance:		Weight loss:	
Average Speed:		Total Hours:	
Average Heart Rate:		Total Burns:	

Notes / Thoughts:

Year: _____ Month: _____ Week: _____ Weekly Goal: _____

Monday	Date:	Burns Target:	
Notes:	Route:		
	Distance:	Time:	
	Weight:	Speed:	
	Burn Cals:	Heart Rate:	
	Weather:	Breathing:	
	How I Felt:		
	Injuries:		
	Overall Thoughts:		

Tuesday	Date:	Burns Target:	
Notes:	Route:		
	Distance:	Time:	
	Weight:	Speed:	
	Burn Cals:	Heart Rate:	
	Weather:	Breathing:	
	How I Felt:		
	Injuries:		
	Overall Thoughts:		

Wednesday	Date:	Burns Target:	
Notes:	Route:		
	Distance:	Time:	
	Weight:	Speed:	
	Burn Cals:	Heart Rate:	
	Weather:	Breathing:	
	How I Felt:		
	Injuries:		
	Overall Thoughts:		

Thursday	Date:	Burns Target:	
Notes:	Route:		
	Distance:	Time:	
	Weight:	Speed:	
	Burn Cals:	Heart Rate:	
	Weather:	Breathing:	
	How I Felt:		
	Injuries:		
	Overall Thoughts:		

Friday	Date:		Burns Target:
Notes:	Route:		
	Distance:		Time:
	Weight:		Speed:
	Burn Cals:		Heart Rate:
	Weather:		Breathing:
	How I Felt:		
	Injuries:		
	Overall Thoughts:		

Saturday	Date:		Burns Target:
Notes:	Route:		
	Distance:		Time:
	Weight:		Speed:
	Burn Cals:		Heart Rate:
	Weather:		Breathing:
	How I Felt:		
	Injuries:		
	Overall Thoughts:		

Sunday	Date:		Burns Target:
Notes:	Route:		
	Distance:		Time:
	Weight:		Speed:
	Burn Cals:		Heart Rate:
	Weather:		Breathing:
	How I Felt:		
	Injuries:		
	Overall Thoughts:		

Weekly Review

Total Distance:		Weight loss:	
Average Speed:		Total Hours:	
Average Heart Rate:		Total Burns:	

Notes / Thoughts:

Year:_____ Month:_____ Week:_____ Weekly Goal:_____

Monday	Date:		Burns Target:
Notes:	Route:		
	Distance:		Time:
	Weight:		Speed:
	Burn Cals:		Heart Rate:
	Weather:		Breathing:
	How I Felt:		
	Injuries:		
	Overall Thoughts:		

Tuesday	Date:		Burns Target:
Notes:	Route:		
	Distance:		Time:
	Weight:		Speed:
	Burn Cals:		Heart Rate:
	Weather:		Breathing:
	How I Felt:		
	Injuries:		
	Overall Thoughts:		

Wednesday	Date:		Burns Target:
Notes:	Route:		
	Distance:		Time:
	Weight:		Speed:
	Burn Cals:		Heart Rate:
	Weather:		Breathing:
	How I Felt:		
	Injuries:		
	Overall Thoughts:		

Thursday	Date:		Burns Target:
Notes:	Route:		
	Distance:		Time:
	Weight:		Speed:
	Burn Cals:		Heart Rate:
	Weather:		Breathing:
	How I Felt:		
	Injuries:		
	Overall Thoughts:		

Friday	Date:		Burns Target:	
Notes:	Route:			
	Distance:		Time:	
	Weight:		Speed:	
	Burn Cals:		Heart Rate:	
	Weather:		Breathing:	
	How I Felt:			
	Injuries:			
	Overall Thoughts:			

Saturday	Date:		Burns Target:	
Notes:	Route:			
	Distance:		Time:	
	Weight:		Speed:	
	Burn Cals:		Heart Rate:	
	Weather:		Breathing:	
	How I Felt:			
	Injuries:			
	Overall Thoughts:			

Sunday	Date:		Burns Target:	
Notes:	Route:			
	Distance:		Time:	
	Weight:		Speed:	
	Burn Cals:		Heart Rate:	
	Weather:		Breathing:	
	How I Felt:			
	Injuries:			
	Overall Thoughts:			

Weekly Review

Total Distance:		Weight loss:	
Average Speed:		Total Hours:	
Average Heart Rate:		Total Burns:	

Notes / Thoughts:

Year:_____ Month:_____ Week:_____ Weekly Goal:_____

Monday	**Date:**		**Burns Target:**
Notes:	Route:		
	Distance:		Time:
	Weight:		Speed:
	Burn Cals:		Heart Rate:
	Weather:		Breathing:
	How I Felt:		
	Injuries:		
	Overall Thoughts:		

Tuesday	**Date:**		**Burns Target:**
Notes:	Route:		
	Distance:		Time:
	Weight:		Speed:
	Burn Cals:		Heart Rate:
	Weather:		Breathing:
	How I Felt:		
	Injuries:		
	Overall Thoughts:		

Wednesday	**Date:**		**Burns Target:**
Notes:	Route:		
	Distance:		Time:
	Weight:		Speed:
	Burn Cals:		Heart Rate:
	Weather:		Breathing:
	How I Felt:		
	Injuries:		
	Overall Thoughts:		

Thursday	**Date:**		**Burns Target:**
Notes:	Route:		
	Distance:		Time:
	Weight:		Speed:
	Burn Cals:		Heart Rate:
	Weather:		Breathing:
	How I Felt:		
	Injuries:		
	Overall Thoughts:		

Friday	**Date:**		**Burns Target:**
Notes:	Route:		
	Distance:		Time:
	Weight:		Speed:
	Burn Cals:		Heart Rate:
	Weather:		Breathing:
	How I Felt:		
	Injuries:		
	Overall Thoughts:		

Saturday	**Date:**		**Burns Target:**
Notes:	Route:		
	Distance:		Time:
	Weight:		Speed:
	Burn Cals:		Heart Rate:
	Weather:		Breathing:
	How I Felt:		
	Injuries:		
	Overall Thoughts:		

Sunday	**Date:**		**Burns Target:**
Notes:	Route:		
	Distance:		Time:
	Weight:		Speed:
	Burn Cals:		Heart Rate:
	Weather:		Breathing:
	How I Felt:		
	Injuries:		
	Overall Thoughts:		

Weekly Review			
Total Distance:		Weight loss:	
Average Speed:		Total Hours:	
Average Heart Rate:		Total Burns:	
Notes / Thoughts:			

Year:........... Month:............ Week:............ Weekly Goal:.........

Monday	**Date:**	**Burns Target:**
Notes:	Route:	
	Distance:	Time:
	Weight:	Speed:
	Burn Cals:	Heart Rate:
	Weather:	Breathing:
	How I Felt:	
	Injuries:	
	Overall Thoughts:	

Tuesday	**Date:**	**Burns Target:**
Notes:	Route:	
	Distance:	Time:
	Weight:	Speed:
	Burn Cals:	Heart Rate:
	Weather:	Breathing:
	How I Felt:	
	Injuries:	
	Overall Thoughts:	

Wednesday	**Date:**	**Burns Target:**
Notes:	Route:	
	Distance:	Time:
	Weight:	Speed:
	Burn Cals:	Heart Rate:
	Weather:	Breathing:
	How I Felt:	
	Injuries:	
	Overall Thoughts:	

Thursday	**Date:**	**Burns Target:**
Notes:	Route:	
	Distance:	Time:
	Weight:	Speed:
	Burn Cals:	Heart Rate:
	Weather:	Breathing:
	How I Felt:	
	Injuries:	
	Overall Thoughts:	

Friday	Date:		Burns Target:	
Notes:	Route:			
	Distance:		Time:	
	Weight:		Speed:	
	Burn Cals:		Heart Rate:	
	Weather:		Breathing:	
	How I Felt:			
	Injuries:			
	Overall Thoughts:			

Saturday	Date:		Burns Target:	
Notes:	Route:			
	Distance:		Time:	
	Weight:		Speed:	
	Burn Cals:		Heart Rate:	
	Weather:		Breathing:	
	How I Felt:			
	Injuries:			
	Overall Thoughts:			

Sunday	Date:		Burns Target:	
Notes:	Route:			
	Distance:		Time:	
	Weight:		Speed:	
	Burn Cals:		Heart Rate:	
	Weather:		Breathing:	
	How I Felt:			
	Injuries:			
	Overall Thoughts:			

Weekly Review

Total Distance:		Weight loss:	
Average Speed:		Total Hours:	
Average Heart Rate:		Total Burns:	

Notes / Thoughts:

Year: _____ Month: _____ Week: _____ Weekly Goal: _____

Monday	Date:		Burns Target:
Notes:	Route:		
	Distance:	Time:	
	Weight:	Speed:	
	Burn Cals:	Heart Rate:	
	Weather:	Breathing:	
	How I Felt:		
	Injuries:		
	Overall Thoughts:		

Tuesday	Date:		Burns Target:
Notes:	Route:		
	Distance:	Time:	
	Weight:	Speed:	
	Burn Cals:	Heart Rate:	
	Weather:	Breathing:	
	How I Felt:		
	Injuries:		
	Overall Thoughts:		

Wednesday	Date:		Burns Target:
Notes:	Route:		
	Distance:	Time:	
	Weight:	Speed:	
	Burn Cals:	Heart Rate:	
	Weather:	Breathing:	
	How I Felt:		
	Injuries:		
	Overall Thoughts:		

Thursday	Date:		Burns Target:
Notes:	Route:		
	Distance:	Time:	
	Weight:	Speed:	
	Burn Cals:	Heart Rate:	
	Weather:	Breathing:	
	How I Felt:		
	Injuries:		
	Overall Thoughts:		

Friday	Date:		Burns Target:	
Notes:	Route:			
	Distance:		Time:	
	Weight:		Speed:	
	Burn Cals:		Heart Rate:	
	Weather:		Breathing:	
	How I Felt:			
	Injuries:			
	Overall Thoughts:			

Saturday	Date:		Burns Target:	
Notes:	Route:			
	Distance:		Time:	
	Weight:		Speed:	
	Burn Cals:		Heart Rate:	
	Weather:		Breathing:	
	How I Felt:			
	Injuries:			
	Overall Thoughts:			

Sunday	Date:		Burns Target:	
Notes:	Route:			
	Distance:		Time:	
	Weight:		Speed:	
	Burn Cals:		Heart Rate:	
	Weather:		Breathing:	
	How I Felt:			
	Injuries:			
	Overall Thoughts:			

Weekly Review

Total Distance:		Weight loss:	
Average Speed:		Total Hours:	
Average Heart Rate:		Total Burns:	

Notes / Thoughts:

Year:_____ Month:_____ Week:_____ Weekly Goal:_____

Monday	Date:		Burns Target:
Notes:	Route:		
	Distance:		Time:
	Weight:		Speed:
	Burn Cals:		Heart Rate:
	Weather:		Breathing:
	How I Felt:		
	Injuries:		
	Overall Thoughts:		

Tuesday	Date:		Burns Target:
Notes:	Route:		
	Distance:		Time:
	Weight:		Speed:
	Burn Cals:		Heart Rate:
	Weather:		Breathing:
	How I Felt:		
	Injuries:		
	Overall Thoughts:		

Wednesday	Date:		Burns Target:
Notes:	Route:		
	Distance:		Time:
	Weight:		Speed:
	Burn Cals:		Heart Rate:
	Weather:		Breathing:
	How I Felt:		
	Injuries:		
	Overall Thoughts:		

Thursday	Date:		Burns Target:
Notes:	Route:		
	Distance:		Time:
	Weight:		Speed:
	Burn Cals:		Heart Rate:
	Weather:		Breathing:
	How I Felt:		
	Injuries:		
	Overall Thoughts:		

Friday	Date:		Burns Target:
Notes:	Route:		
	Distance:		Time:
	Weight:		Speed:
	Burn Cals:		Heart Rate:
	Weather:		Breathing:
	How I Felt:		
	Injuries:		
	Overall Thoughts:		

Saturday	Date:		Burns Target:
Notes:	Route:		
	Distance:		Time:
	Weight:		Speed:
	Burn Cals:		Heart Rate:
	Weather:		Breathing:
	How I Felt:		
	Injuries:		
	Overall Thoughts:		

Sunday	Date:		Burns Target:
Notes:	Route:		
	Distance:		Time:
	Weight:		Speed:
	Burn Cals:		Heart Rate:
	Weather:		Breathing:
	How I Felt:		
	Injuries:		
	Overall Thoughts:		

Weekly Review

Total Distance:		Weight loss:	
Average Speed:		Total Hours:	
Average Heart Rate:		Total Burns:	

Notes / Thoughts:

Year: .... Month: .... Week: .... Weekly Goal: ....

Monday	Date:	Burns Target:
Notes:	Route:	
	Distance:	Time:
	Weight:	Speed:
	Burn Cals:	Heart Rate:
	Weather:	Breathing:
	How I Felt:	
	Injuries:	
	Overall Thoughts:	

Tuesday	Date:	Burns Target:
Notes:	Route:	
	Distance:	Time:
	Weight:	Speed:
	Burn Cals:	Heart Rate:
	Weather:	Breathing:
	How I Felt:	
	Injuries:	
	Overall Thoughts:	

Wednesday	Date:	Burns Target:
Notes:	Route:	
	Distance:	Time:
	Weight:	Speed:
	Burn Cals:	Heart Rate:
	Weather:	Breathing:
	How I Felt:	
	Injuries:	
	Overall Thoughts:	

Thursday	Date:	Burns Target:
Notes:	Route:	
	Distance:	Time:
	Weight:	Speed:
	Burn Cals:	Heart Rate:
	Weather:	Breathing:
	How I Felt:	
	Injuries:	
	Overall Thoughts:	

Friday	Date:		Burns Target:	
Notes:	Route:			
	Distance:		Time:	
	Weight:		Speed:	
	Burn Cals:		Heart Rate:	
	Weather:		Breathing:	
	How I Felt:			
	Injuries:			
	Overall Thoughts:			

Saturday	Date:		Burns Target:	
Notes:	Route:			
	Distance:		Time:	
	Weight:		Speed:	
	Burn Cals:		Heart Rate:	
	Weather:		Breathing:	
	How I Felt:			
	Injuries:			
	Overall Thoughts:			

Sunday	Date:		Burns Target:	
Notes:	Route:			
	Distance:		Time:	
	Weight:		Speed:	
	Burn Cals:		Heart Rate:	
	Weather:		Breathing:	
	How I Felt:			
	Injuries:			
	Overall Thoughts:			

Weekly Review

Total Distance:		Weight loss:	
Average Speed:		Total Hours:	
Average Heart Rate:		Total Burns:	

Notes / Thoughts:

Year: .... Month: .... Week: .... Weekly Goal: ....

Monday	**Date:**	**Burns Target:**
Notes:	Route:	
	Distance:	Time:
	Weight:	Speed:
	Burn Cals:	Heart Rate:
	Weather:	Breathing:
	How I Felt:	
	Injuries:	
	Overall Thoughts:	

Tuesday	**Date:**	**Burns Target:**
Notes:	Route:	
	Distance:	Time:
	Weight:	Speed:
	Burn Cals:	Heart Rate:
	Weather:	Breathing:
	How I Felt:	
	Injuries:	
	Overall Thoughts:	

Wednesday	**Date:**	**Burns Target:**
Notes:	Route:	
	Distance:	Time:
	Weight:	Speed:
	Burn Cals:	Heart Rate:
	Weather:	Breathing:
	How I Felt:	
	Injuries:	
	Overall Thoughts:	

Thursday	**Date:**	**Burns Target:**
Notes:	Route:	
	Distance:	Time:
	Weight:	Speed:
	Burn Cals:	Heart Rate:
	Weather:	Breathing:
	How I Felt:	
	Injuries:	
	Overall Thoughts:	

Friday	Date:		Burns Target:	
Notes:	Route:			
	Distance:		Time:	
	Weight:		Speed:	
	Burn Cals:		Heart Rate:	
	Weather:		Breathing:	
	How I Felt:			
	Injuries:			
	Overall Thoughts:			

Saturday	Date:		Burns Target:	
Notes:	Route:			
	Distance:		Time:	
	Weight:		Speed:	
	Burn Cals:		Heart Rate:	
	Weather:		Breathing:	
	How I Felt:			
	Injuries:			
	Overall Thoughts:			

Sunday	Date:		Burns Target:	
Notes:	Route:			
	Distance:		Time:	
	Weight:		Speed:	
	Burn Cals:		Heart Rate:	
	Weather:		Breathing:	
	How I Felt:			
	Injuries:			
	Overall Thoughts:			

Weekly Review

Total Distance:		Weight loss:	
Average Speed:		Total Hours:	
Average Heart Rate:		Total Burns:	

Notes / Thoughts:

Year: _____ Month: _____ Week: _____ Weekly Goal: _____

Monday	Date:	Burns Target:
Notes:	Route:	
	Distance:	Time:
	Weight:	Speed:
	Burn Cals:	Heart Rate:
	Weather:	Breathing:
	How I Felt:	
	Injuries:	
	Overall Thoughts:	

Tuesday	Date:	Burns Target:
Notes:	Route:	
	Distance:	Time:
	Weight:	Speed:
	Burn Cals:	Heart Rate:
	Weather:	Breathing:
	How I Felt:	
	Injuries:	
	Overall Thoughts:	

Wednesday	Date:	Burns Target:
Notes:	Route:	
	Distance:	Time:
	Weight:	Speed:
	Burn Cals:	Heart Rate:
	Weather:	Breathing:
	How I Felt:	
	Injuries:	
	Overall Thoughts:	

Thursday	Date:	Burns Target:
Notes:	Route:	
	Distance:	Time:
	Weight:	Speed:
	Burn Cals:	Heart Rate:
	Weather:	Breathing:
	How I Felt:	
	Injuries:	
	Overall Thoughts:	

Friday	Date:		Burns Target:
Notes:	Route:		
	Distance:	Time:	
	Weight:	Speed:	
	Burn Cals:	Heart Rate:	
	Weather:	Breathing:	
	How I Felt:		
	Injuries:		
	Overall Thoughts:		

Saturday	Date:		Burns Target:
Notes:	Route:		
	Distance:	Time:	
	Weight:	Speed:	
	Burn Cals:	Heart Rate:	
	Weather:	Breathing:	
	How I Felt:		
	Injuries:		
	Overall Thoughts:		

Sunday	Date:		Burns Target:
Notes:	Route:		
	Distance:	Time:	
	Weight:	Speed:	
	Burn Cals:	Heart Rate:	
	Weather:	Breathing:	
	How I Felt:		
	Injuries:		
	Overall Thoughts:		

Weekly Review

Total Distance:		Weight loss:	
Average Speed:		Total Hours:	
Average Heart Rate:		Total Burns:	

Notes / Thoughts:

Year: _____ Month: _____ Week: _____ Weekly Goal: _____

Monday	**Date:**	**Burns Target:**
Notes:	Route:	
	Distance:	Time:
	Weight:	Speed:
	Burn Cals:	Heart Rate:
	Weather:	Breathing:
	How I Felt:	
	Injuries:	
	Overall Thoughts:	

Tuesday	**Date:**	**Burns Target:**
Notes:	Route:	
	Distance:	Time:
	Weight:	Speed:
	Burn Cals:	Heart Rate:
	Weather:	Breathing:
	How I Felt:	
	Injuries:	
	Overall Thoughts:	

Wednesday	**Date:**	**Burns Target:**
Notes:	Route:	
	Distance:	Time:
	Weight:	Speed:
	Burn Cals:	Heart Rate:
	Weather:	Breathing:
	How I Felt:	
	Injuries:	
	Overall Thoughts:	

Thursday	**Date:**	**Burns Target:**
Notes:	Route:	
	Distance:	Time:
	Weight:	Speed:
	Burn Cals:	Heart Rate:
	Weather:	Breathing:
	How I Felt:	
	Injuries:	
	Overall Thoughts:	

Friday	Date:	Burns Target:	
Notes:	Route:		
	Distance:	Time:	
	Weight:	Speed:	
	Burn Cals:	Heart Rate:	
	Weather:	Breathing:	
	How I Felt:		
	Injuries:		
	Overall Thoughts:		

Saturday	Date:	Burns Target:	
Notes:	Route:		
	Distance:	Time:	
	Weight:	Speed:	
	Burn Cals:	Heart Rate:	
	Weather:	Breathing:	
	How I Felt:		
	Injuries:		
	Overall Thoughts:		

Sunday	Date:	Burns Target:	
Notes:	Route:		
	Distance:	Time:	
	Weight:	Speed:	
	Burn Cals:	Heart Rate:	
	Weather:	Breathing:	
	How I Felt:		
	Injuries:		
	Overall Thoughts:		

Weekly Review

Total Distance:		Weight loss:	
Average Speed:		Total Hours:	
Average Heart Rate:		Total Burns:	

Notes / Thoughts:

Year:_____ Month:_____ Week:_____ Weekly Goal:_____

Monday	Date:	Burns Target:
Notes:	Route:	
	Distance:	Time:
	Weight:	Speed:
	Burn Cals:	Heart Rate:
	Weather:	Breathing:
	How I Felt:	
	Injuries:	
	Overall Thoughts:	

Tuesday	Date:	Burns Target:
Notes:	Route:	
	Distance:	Time:
	Weight:	Speed:
	Burn Cals:	Heart Rate:
	Weather:	Breathing:
	How I Felt:	
	Injuries:	
	Overall Thoughts:	

Wednesday	Date:	Burns Target:
Notes:	Route:	
	Distance:	Time:
	Weight:	Speed:
	Burn Cals:	Heart Rate:
	Weather:	Breathing:
	How I Felt:	
	Injuries:	
	Overall Thoughts:	

Thursday	Date:	Burns Target:
Notes:	Route:	
	Distance:	Time:
	Weight:	Speed:
	Burn Cals:	Heart Rate:
	Weather:	Breathing:
	How I Felt:	
	Injuries:	
	Overall Thoughts:	

Friday	Date:			Burns Target:	
Notes:	Route:				
	Distance:		Time:		
	Weight:		Speed:		
	Burn Cals:		Heart Rate:		
	Weather:		Breathing:		
	How I Felt:				
	Injuries:				
	Overall Thoughts:				

Saturday	Date:			Burns Target:	
Notes:	Route:				
	Distance:		Time:		
	Weight:		Speed:		
	Burn Cals:		Heart Rate:		
	Weather:		Breathing:		
	How I Felt:				
	Injuries:				
	Overall Thoughts:				

Sunday	Date:			Burns Target:	
Notes:	Route:				
	Distance:		Time:		
	Weight:		Speed:		
	Burn Cals:		Heart Rate:		
	Weather:		Breathing:		
	How I Felt:				
	Injuries:				
	Overall Thoughts:				

Weekly Review

Total Distance:		Weight loss:	
Average Speed:		Total Hours:	
Average Heart Rate:		Total Burns:	

Notes / Thoughts:

Year:_____ Month:_____ Week:_____ Weekly Goal:_____

Monday	Date:	Burns Target:
Notes:	Route:	
	Distance:	Time:
	Weight:	Speed:
	Burn Cals:	Heart Rate:
	Weather:	Breathing:
	How I Felt:	
	Injuries:	
	Overall Thoughts:	

Tuesday	Date:	Burns Target:
Notes:	Route:	
	Distance:	Time:
	Weight:	Speed:
	Burn Cals:	Heart Rate:
	Weather:	Breathing:
	How I Felt:	
	Injuries:	
	Overall Thoughts:	

Wednesday	Date:	Burns Target:
Notes:	Route:	
	Distance:	Time:
	Weight:	Speed:
	Burn Cals:	Heart Rate:
	Weather:	Breathing:
	How I Felt:	
	Injuries:	
	Overall Thoughts:	

Thursday	Date:	Burns Target:
Notes:	Route:	
	Distance:	Time:
	Weight:	Speed:
	Burn Cals:	Heart Rate:
	Weather:	Breathing:
	How I Felt:	
	Injuries:	
	Overall Thoughts:	

Friday	Date:	Burns Target:
Notes:	Route:	
	Distance:	Time:
	Weight:	Speed:
	Burn Cals:	Heart Rate:
	Weather:	Breathing:
	How I Felt:	
	Injuries:	
	Overall Thoughts:	

Saturday	Date:	Burns Target:
Notes:	Route:	
	Distance:	Time:
	Weight:	Speed:
	Burn Cals:	Heart Rate:
	Weather:	Breathing:
	How I Felt:	
	Injuries:	
	Overall Thoughts:	

Sunday	Date:	Burns Target:
Notes:	Route:	
	Distance:	Time:
	Weight:	Speed:
	Burn Cals:	Heart Rate:
	Weather:	Breathing:
	How I Felt:	
	Injuries:	
	Overall Thoughts:	

Weekly Review

Total Distance:		Weight loss:	
Average Speed:		Total Hours:	
Average Heart Rate:		Total Burns:	

Notes / Thoughts:

Made in the USA
Monee, IL
04 October 2022

15259987R00059